THE BOOK OF
KNITTED TOYS

ROBYN EARL-PEACOCK

an ABC BOOK

CONTENTS

About this book 4
Abbreviations 4
Useful Information 5
Play School 6
Big Ted 8
Jemima 12
Humpty 16
Banana in Pyjamas 20
Baby Teddy Bear 23
Slush 24
Daisy 27
Fido 29
Johnson & friends 32
McDuff 33
Johnson 36
Alfred 40
Raggy Dolls 44
Sad Sack 45
Princess 48
Back-to-Front 52
Mr Squiggle 57
Inspector Gadget 61
Postman Pat and Jess 67
David the Gnome and Lisa 72

The patterns in this book are for the use of private individuals only and they may not be used for any commercial purposes without the prior written consent of ABC Enterprises.

ABOUT THIS BOOK

The idea for creating a knitting book of soft toys originally arose out of my love of knitting and my children's love of soft cuddly toys. When the ABC provided me with the concept of producing a book of ABC children's program characters, I was enthralled with having to create knitting patterns for all those wonderful, colourful and much-loved familiar toys.

Whether from *Play School*, *Johnson & friends*, or the ever-popular *Mr Squiggle*, these toys are sure to delight all children, simply because they know the characters and they are already a favourite part of their lives.

Adults will find the characters fun to knit and the easy-to-follow patterns, each with a designated degree of difficulty, will ensure that even the most inexperienced knitter is able to produce a soft, cuddly toy any child will love.

A number of people were indispensible in writing this book: I would like to thank my sister, Dorothy, who painstakingly typed my scribble; my brother, Glenn, who collated and edited it; and Jayne Denshire of ABC Enterprises, who helped make my first publishing venture an enjoyable and rewarding experience.

Many thanks must go to my husband, Glenn, for his unquestioning belief in my abilities and to my two small daughters, Skye and Ashe, whose intimate knowledge of every character was invaluable. To all my friends and family who encouraged and enthused me over each creation I am considerably indebted.

My greatest thanks must go to my mother, Dorothy Hamilton, who first imparted to me this treasured knowledge—the joy of knitting.

Robyn Earl-Peacock

ABBREVIATIONS

Knitting
alt.	alternate
beg.	beginning
cont.	continue, continuing
foll.	following
dec(s).	decrease, decreasings: work 2 stitches together
g. st	garter stitch: every row knit
inc.	increase: work into front, then back of same stitch and pull the 2 loops off together
K	knit
L.H.	left hand
m.2	lift loop lying between the last and the next sts. Place on L.H. needles. Work into the front and then the back
P	purl
P.S.S.O.	pass slip stitch over
rem.	remain, remaining
rpt	repeat
R.H.	right hand
R.S.	right side
sl.	slip
st(s)	stitch(es)
st.st	stocking stitch: one row knit, one row purl
t.b.l.	through back of loop
tog.	together
W.S.	wrong side
y. fwd	yarn forward

Crochet
ch.	chain
dc	double crochet
rnd	round
sl. st	slip stitch

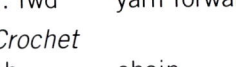

Useful Information

Tension

Tension is not important when knitting toys as it does not matter if the finished article is slightly larger or smaller than that size given in the pattern. The following tension chart is given as a general guide only. Using 3.25 mm knitting needles and 8-ply yarn, 10 sts over 20 g. st rows measures 4.5 cm square.

Sewing Seams

When sewing two g. st pieces together, use an overstitch. When sewing two st.st pieces together, use a fine backstitch.

Changing Colours in the Middle of a Row

Always pull yarn to the wrong side of the work, bring colour to be worked under, then over the colour just completed.

To Make a Twisted Cord

Cut a length of yarn approx. 150 cm long. Fold in half and, holding each end firmly, twist, until when folded again it will twist around itself. Tie off each end and trim neatly.

Needle Sizes Used

Imperial	Metric
11	3.00 mm
10	3.25 mm

Crochet Hook Sizes Used

Imperial	Metric
9	3.5 mm

To Fill Knitted Toys

To ensure the toys hold their shape and show their true characteristic features, they need to be filled very firmly, making sure the filling is pushed to the front and back of the toy as well as the sides.

To Make a Small Pompon

Cut two circles from cardboard, approx. 30 mm in diameter. Cut a centre hole in each approx. 10 mm in diameter. Place the two circles together and with long strands of yarn (two at a time is quicker) lace through the centre hole over the outer edge and back through the centre hole. Continue working around the two pieces of cardboard until the centre hole is filled. A number of strands may be required. Holding the centre firmly, cut through the yarn around the outer edge. Wrap a length of yarn around the centre between the two pieces of cardboard and tie firmly. Slide the two pieces of cardboard off each side. Shake the pompon gently to remove any loose fibres.

Difficulty Rating

* Easy knitting at beginner level with simple shaping.
** Some experience necessary with slightly more complicated shaping.
*** Advanced knitting with some complicated shaping.
C Some crochet involved although all crochet is at beginner level.

PLAY SCHOOL

This long-time favourite program is sure to be a winner with any preschooler you know. Whether joining in with the toys and presenters, or waiting for the story clock to turn, young children are informed, amused and entertained by *Play School*—day after day.

BIG TED

Big Ted is a real favourite among the toys on *Play School*. You can now have your own cuddly version of this toy which has been part of *Play School* for more than twenty years.

BIG TED **C

DESCRIPTION

Legs, body and head are knitted in two pieces, one for the front and one for the back. Base of feet, arms, ears and muzzle are knitted in one piece each. Nose is crocheted. When completed he stands approx. 48 cm high.

MATERIALS

Three 50 g balls gold mohair 8-ply yarn
One 20 g ball gold 8-ply yarn
Small quantity black 8-ply yarn
One pair 15 mm animal safety eyes
One pair 3.25 mm knitting needles
One 3.5 mm crochet hook
Tapestry needle
Polyester fibre filling

ABBREVIATIONS

See page 4.

FRONT

With 3.25 mm knitting needles, gold mohair yarn and beg. with right foot, cast on 15 sts.
Inc. K wise in every st—30 sts.
K 14 rows.
K2 tog. across row—15 sts.
K 24 rows.
*Break yarn and leave sts on needle. Work another leg the same. *Do not break yarn.*

To Shape Body

K 2 rows across both legs—30 sts.
Next row K1, (inc. in next st, K2) to last 2 sts, inc. in next st, K1—40 sts.
K 9 rows.
Dec. at each end of next and foll. 10th rows till 30 sts rem.
K 19 rows.
Cast off 4 sts at beg. of next 2 rows, then 3 sts at beg. of foll. 2 rows—16 st.

To Shape Head

Next row (Inc. in next st) twice, (K1,. inc. in next st) 3 times, (inc. in next st, K1) 3 times, (inc. in next st) twice—26 sts.
K 1 row.
Inc. at each end of next and foll. alt. rows till 34 sts.
K 35 rows.
Dec. at each end of next and foll. alt. rows till 28 sts rem.
K 1 row.
Next row (K2 tog., K1) 4 times, (K2 tog.) twice, (K1, K2 tog.) 4 times—18 sts.
Cast off.

BACK

With 3.25 mm knitting needles, gold mohair yarn, and beg. with left foot, cast on 10 sts.
Row 1 (K1, inc. in next st) to end—15 sts.
K 39 rows.
Cont. as for front from *.

RIGHT ARM

With 3.25 mm knitting needles, gold mohair yarn and beg. at end of paw, cast on 10 sts.
Inc. K wise in every st—20 sts.
Rpt this row once—40 sts.
K 16 rows.*
Next row K4, (K2 tog., K1) 9 times, K9—31 sts.
**K 25 rows.
Cast off 2 sts at beg. of next 2 rows—27 sts.
Dec. at each end of every row till 3 sts rem.
Cast off.

LEFT ARM

Work as for right arm to *.
Next row K10, (K2 tog., K1) 9 times, K3—31 sts.
Complete as for right arm from **.

BIG TED

BASE OF FEET (*make 2*)

With 3.25 mm knitting needles and gold yarn, cast on 5 sts.
Working in st.st inc. at each end of every row till 13 sts.
St.st 8 rows.
Dec. at each end of every row till 3 sts rem.
Cast off P wise.

EARS (*make 2*)

With 3.25 mm knitting needles and gold mohair yarn, cast on 4 sts.

Row 1 Inc. in every st—8 sts.

Next and foll. alt. rows K.

Row 3 K1, (inc. in next st) twice, K2, (inc. in next st) twice, K1.

Row 5 K3, (inc. in next st) twice, K2, (inc. in next st) twice, K3.

Row 7 K5, (inc. in next st) twice, K2, (inc. in next st) twice, K5.
Cont. working in this way, knitting 2 extra sts at each end of needle on alt. rows till 40 sts.

Rows 18–20 K.

Row 21 K15, (K2 tog.) twice, K2, (K2 tog. t.b.l.) twice, K15.

Row 23 K13, (K2 tog.) twice, K2, (K2 tog. t.b.l.) twice, K13.

Row 25 K11, (K2 tog.) twice, K2, (K2 tog. t.b.l.) twice, K11.

Row 26 K
Break off gold mohair yarn and join in gold yarn for front ear piece.

Row 27 K9, (K2 tog.) twice, K2, (K2 tog. t.b.l.) twice, K9.

Next and foll. alt. rows P.

Row 29 K7, (K2 tog.) twice, K2, (K2 tog. t.b.l.) twice, K7.
Cont. working in this way, knitting 2 fewer sts at each end of needle on alt. rows till 8 sts rem.

Row 36 P.

Row 37 (K2 tog.) twice, (K2 tog. t.b.l.) twice—4 sts.
Cast off P wise.

MUZZLE

With 3.25 mm knitting needles and gold mohair yarn, cast on 48 sts.
K 1 row (R.S. facing).

Row 2 K10, (K2 tog.) twice, K20, (K2 tog.) twice, K10.

Next and foll. alt. rows K.

Row 4 K9, (K2 tog.) twice, K18, (K2 tog.) twice, K9.

Row 6 K8, (K2 tog.) twice, K16, (K2 tog.) twice, K8.
Cont. working in this way, reducing sts on either side of decreasings on alt. rows till 20 sts rem.

Row 15 K.

Row 16 K2 tog. across row—10 sts.
Break yarn leaving a long end.
Thread it through rem. sts and pull firmly. Tie off.

NOSE

With 3.5 mm crochet hook and black yarn, make 2 ch.

Rnd 1 Work 6 dc in 2nd ch. from hook.

Rnd 2 Work 2 dc in each dc around—12 dc.

Rnd 3 (Work 1 dc in next dc then 2 dc in next dc). Rpt to end of rnd—18 dc.
Sl. st in next dc. Fasten off.

BIG TED

To Make Up

Body

Attach animal safety eyes to front head section. Position carefully slightly below centre line.
With right sides together, sew seam down each side of the head, body and legs. Sew inner leg seams. Leave base of feet and cast-off edges at top of head open.
Place the right sides of base of foot and bottom of leg together, matching cast-on edge of base to back of foot. Sew seam around. Complete other leg to match.
Turn to right side and fill firmly. Sew cast-off edges at top of head together.

Arms

Fold in half lengthwise and sew seam from cast-on edge to armhole. Position seam in centre at cast-on edge and sew across end of paw. Turn to right side and fill firmly. With the seam at centre front and matching top of arm to shoulder shaping, sl. st around armhole shaping. Complete other arm to match.

Ears

Fold in half so that wrong sides are together. Fill firmly and sew cast-off and cast-on edges together at centre. Sl. st in position, placing the front edge slightly forward of the head seam and the back edge slightly behind the head seam. Complete other ear to match.

Muzzle

Fold right sides together and sew seam from centre to cast-on edge. Turn to right side and fill firmly. With seam at centre bottom and top edge in line with the bottom of the eyes, sl. st to face around cast-on edge. Run a length of yarn around neck and pull slightly to shape. Tie off.

Nose

Run a length of yarn around outer edge of nose piece. Pull slightly and fill firmly. Cont. to pull yarn till a ball is formed. Tie off.
With bottom edge at centre of muzzle, sl. st in position.

Mouth

With black yarn and using a long stitch embroider mouth as illustrated.
Brush the mohair gently to make it fluffy.

casting on

casting off

JEMIMA

Jemima's knitted overalls and wool hair make her *Play School*'s most loveable little rag doll. She has her own outfit for special occasions too.

Description

Legs, body and head are knitted in two pieces, one for the front and one for the back. Arms are knitted in one piece each. Eyes, mouth and cheeks are embroidered. Overalls are knitted in four pieces—front, back and braces, and dress in five pieces—front, back, sleeves and pocket. When completed she stands approx. 32 cm tall.

Materials

Body

One 50 g ball bone 8-ply yarn
One 25 g ball red 8-ply yarn
One 20 g ball black 8-ply yarn
One 50 g ball black 12-ply yarn
Small quantity crimson 8-ply yarn

Overalls

One 25 g ball dark green 8-ply yarn
Four small white buttons

JEMIMA

Dress

One 50 g ball mauve 8-ply yarn
Three small mauve buttons
Five stitch holders
Length of narrow white lace
Length of narrow mauve ribbon for hair
One pair 3.25 mm knitting needles
Tapestry needle
Polyester fibre filling

ABBREVIATIONS

See page 4.

FRONT

With 3.25 mm knitting needles, black 8-ply yarn and beg. with right shoe, cast on 4 sts.

Row 1 Inc. K wise in every st—8 sts.

Row 2 Inc. P wise in every st—16 sts.
St.st 8 rows.
Break off black yarn and join in bone yarn for leg.

Next row K2 tog. across row—8 sts.
Beg. with a P row, st.st 31 rows.
*Break yarn and leave sts on needle.
Work another leg the same. *Do not break yarn.*

To Shape Body

Next row (Inc. in 1st st, K6, inc. in next st), rpt across 2nd leg—20 sts.
Cont. in st.st working 11 rows across both legs.
Break off bone yarn and join in red yarn for T-shirt.
St.st 14 rows.

To Shape Shoulders

Dec. at each end of every row till 8 sts rem.
K 2 rows.
Break off red yarn and join in bone yarn for head.

To Shape Head

Inc. at each end of every row till 20 sts.
St.st 18 rows.
Dec. at each end of every row till 10 sts rem. Cast off P wise.

BACK

With 3.25 mm knitting needles, black 8-ply yarn and beg. with left shoe, cast on 4 sts.
Inc. K wise in every st—8 sts.
Beg. with a P row, st.st 9 rows.
Break off black yarn and join in bone yarn for leg.
St.st 32 rows.
Complete as for front from *.

ARMS (*make 2*)

With 3.25 mm knitting needles and bone yarn, cast on 8 sts.
Inc. K wise in every st—16 sts.
Beg. with a P row, st.st 5 rows.
Dec. at each end of next row—14 sts.
St.st 15 rows.
Break off bone yarn and join in red yarn for sleeves.
K 4 rows.
Working in st.st, cast off 2 sts at beg. of next 2 rows—10 sts.
Dec. at each end of next and foll. alt. rows till 2 sts rem. P 2 tog. Fasten off.

OVERALLS—FRONT

*With 3.25 mm knitting needles, dark green yarn and beg. with right leg, cast on 15 sts.
K 3 rows.
Beg. with a K row, st.st 26 rows.
Break yarn and leave sts on R.H. needle.
Work another leg the same. *Do not break yarn.*
Cont. in st.st, working 10 rows across both legs—30 sts.

Next row K.

Next row K2, P26, K2.
Rpt last 2 rows once then K one row.

Next row K2, P2, (P2 tog., P2) 6 times, K2—24sts.**

13

Jemima

To Shape Waistband

K 2 rows.

Buttonhole row K2, y. fwd, K2 tog., K17, y. fwd, K2 tog., K1.
K 1 row.

To Shape Bib

Cast off 5 sts, K13, turn.
Cont. to work on these 14 sts only.

Next row K2, P10, K2.

Next row K.
Rpt last 2 rows 5 times.
K 1 row.

Buttonhole row K2, y. fwd, K2 tog., K7, y. fwd, K2 tog., K1.
K 1 row. Cast off.
Ret. to rem. 5 sts. Join in yarn. Cast off.

Overalls—Back

Work as for front from * to **.
K 4 rows. Cast off.

Braces (make 2)

With 3.25 mm knitting needles and dark green yarn, cast on 30 sts. Cast off.

Dress—Front

With 3.25 mm knitting needles, mauve yarn and beg. at hemline, cast on 44 sts.
K 1 row.
Beg. with a K row, st.st 30 rows.

To Shape Waistband

Next row K2 tog. across row—22 sts.
K 3 rows.
Cont. in st.st, inc. at each end of next row—24 sts.
P 1 row.

To Shape Armholes

Cast off 2 sts at beg. of next 2 rows—20 sts.
Dec. at each end of next and foll. 4th rows till 10 sts rem.
P 1 row. Leave on st holder.

Dress—Back

With 3.25 mm knitting needles, mauve yarn and beg. at hemline, cast on 44 sts.
K 1 row.
Beg. with a K row, st.st 20 rows.

Divide for Back Opening

Next row K22 turn.

Next row K2, P to end.
Rpt last 2 rows 4 times.

To Shape Waistband

Next row K2 tog. across row—11 sts.
K 1 row.

Buttonhole row K8, y. fwd, K2 tog., K1.
K 1 row.
Cont. in st.st, inc. at beg. of next row—12 sts.

Next row K2, P10.

To Shape Armhole

Row 1 Cast off 2 sts, K to end.

Row 2 K2, P to end.

Row 3 K2 tog., K to end.

Row 4 K2, P to end.

Row 5 K.
Rpt rows 2, 3, 4, once.

Row 9 (buttonhole row) K to last 3 sts, y. fwd, K2 tog., K1.
Rpt rows 2, 3, 4, 5 twice, then rows 2, 3, 4 once—5 sts.
Leave sts on stitch holder.
Ret. to rem. 22 sts and work to correspond with right side, reversing shaping and omitting buttonholes.

Sleeves (make 2)

With 3.25 mm knitting needles and mauve yarn, cast on 16 sts.
K 1 row.

Next row (K1, inc. in next st) to end—24 sts.
Beg. with a P row, st.st 3 rows.

To Shape Armholes

Cast off 2 sts at beg. of next 2 rows—20 sts.

JEMIMA

Dec. at each end of next and foll. alt. rows till 2 sts rem.
P 1 row. Leave on st holder.

NECK BAND

First, with right sides together sew in raglan sleeves to front and back shapings, sew underarm and side seams.
Then, beg. at right back, slip 5 sts from back, 2 sts from sleeve, 10 sts from front, 2 sts from sleeve and 5 sts from left back onto needle—24 sts. R.S. facing.

Row 1 (buttonhole row) K to last 3 sts, y. fwd, K2 tog., K1.

Row 2 K.
Cast off loosely.

POCKET

With 3.25 mm knitting needles and mauve yarn, cast on 4 sts.
Working in st.st inc. at each end of every row till 12 sts.
St.st 7 rows.

Next row K2 tog. across row—6 sts. Cast off.

TO MAKE UP

Body

With right sides together, sew seams down each side of the head, body and legs, inside leg seams and along cast-on edges at base of shoes. Leave cast-off edges at top of head open. Turn to right side and fill legs firmly. With a fine back st sew across top of legs pulling front to back firmly. This will keep the legs movable. Cont. to fill body and head. Sew cast-off edges at top of head together.

Arms

Fold one arm in half lengthwise with right sides together and sew side seam from armhole shaping to end of arm and across cast-on edges at hand. Turn to right side and fill firmly. Sl. st armhole shaping to body matching the top point approx. 1 cm down from neckband.
Run lengths of yarn around wrists and pull firmly to shape hand. Tie off. To shape thumb, run yarn from inside top edge of hand to centre of hand and pull firmly. Tie off.
Run lengths of yarn around waist and ankles, pull firmly to shape. Tie off.

Face

With black 8-ply yarn embroider eyes in satin stitch and mouth in red backstitch. With crimson yarn embroider cheeks by following the stitch lines as illustrated.

Hair

Cut lengths of black 12-ply yarn approx. 25 cm long. Beg. just in front of top of head seam, thread 3 strands of yarn through centre stitch. Cont. working in this way from front, over top and down back of head to approx. 1 cm from neckband. Work backstitch down this centre line to secure strands. Run lengths of yarn from front to back over all strands to form parting. Thread a length of yarn through side seam just below the cheek line and tie bunch securely to the side of the head. Complete other side to match. Trim hair to length.

Overalls

With right sides together, sew back to front down each side of legs, leaving sides open from g. st shaping to waistband. Sew inside leg seams. Turn to right side. Sew buttons in position at each end of back waistband and at one end of each braces strap. Cross braces at back and sew ends to back waistband.

Dress

Sew on buttons. With a fine running st and gathering slightly as you go, sew lace around neckline, cuffs and pocket as illustrated. Sl. st pocket in position. Tie ribbon around bunches of hair.

Humpty

Humpty, from *Play School*, is the most huggable egg you will find. His spotted vest and cheeky features are all created as you go.

HUMPTY *C

DESCRIPTION

Body is knitted in two identical pieces—one for the front and one for the back. Arms and legs are knitted in one piece each. Collar, bow tie and lips are knitted. Nose, eyes and 'red spots' are crocheted.
When completed he sits approx. 22 cm high.

MATERIALS

One 100 g ball bone 8-ply yarn
One 25 g ball red 8-ply yarn
One 20 g ball green 8-ply yarn
One 20 g ball white 8-ply yarn
Small quantities black 8-ply yarn and black 12-ply yarn
One pair 3.25 mm knitting needles
One 3.5 mm crochet hook
Tapestry needle
Polyester fibre filling

ABBREVIATIONS

See page 4.

BODY (*make 2*)

With 3.25 mm knitting needles and bone yarn, cast on 20 sts.
Working in st.st, inc. at each end of every row till 44 sts.
Work 60 rows straight.
Dec. at each end of every row till 20 sts rem.
Cast off.

LEGS (*make 2*)

With 3.25 mm knitting needles, bone yarn and commencing at sole of foot, cast on 36 sts.
Work in st.st for 8 rows.

To Shape Instep

Row 1 K16, K2 tog. twice, K16.

Row 2 P15, P2 tog. twice, P15.
Cont. in this manner, working one less st on either side of decs. on every foll. row till 24 sts rem.
Work 30 rows straight. Cast off.

ARMS (*make 2*)

With 3.25 mm knitting needles and bone yarn and commencing at end of hand, cast on 8 sts.
Work in st.st.

To Shape Hand

Row 1 Inc. in 1st st, K2, (inc. in next st) twice, K2, inc. in last st—12 sts.

Row 2 Inc. in 1st st, P4, (inc. in next st) twice, P4, inc. in last st—16 sts.

Row 3 Inc. in 1st st, K6, (inc. in next st) twice, K6, inc. in last st—20 sts.

Row 4 Inc. in 1st st, P8, (inc. in next st) twice, P8, inc. in last st—24 sts.
Work 2 rows straight.

Row 7 K11, (inc. in next st) twice, K11—26 sts.

Row 8 P12, (inc. in next st) twice, P12—28 sts.

Row 9 K13, (inc. in next st) twice, K13—30 sts.

Row 10 P14, (inc. in next st) twice, P14—32 sts.
Work 2 rows straight.

Row 13 K2 tog., K12, (K2 tog.) twice, K12, K2 tog.—28 sts.

Row 14 P12, (P2 tog.) twice, P12—26 sts.

Row 15 K2 tog., K9, (K2 tog.) twice, K9, K2 tog—22 sts.

Row 16 P9, (P2 tog.) twice, P9—20 sts.
Work 24 rows straight. Cast off.

HUMPTY

COLLAR

With 3.25 mm knitting needles and green yarn, cast on 80 sts. K 1 row. Working in g. st, inc. at each end of every row till 88 sts.
K 6 rows.
Break off green yarn and join in white yarn.
Dec. at each end of every row till 80 sts rem.
K 1 row. Cast off.

BOW TIE (*make 2 pieces*)

With 3.25 mm knitting needles and red yarn, cast on 30 sts. K 2 rows. Cast off.

SPOTS (*make 14*)

With 3.5 mm crochet hook and red yarn, make 2 ch.

Rnd 1 Work 6 dc in 2nd ch. from hook.

Rnd 2 Work 2 dc in each dc around—12dc.

Rnd 3 (Work 1 dc in next dc then 2 dc in 2nd dc.) Rpt to end of row—18 dc.
Sl. st in next dc. Fasten off.

NOSE

With 3.5 mm crochet hook and white yarn make 2 ch.

Rnd 1 Work 6 dc in 2nd dc from hook.

Rnd 2 Work 2 dc in each dc around—12dc.

Rnd 3 (Work 1 dc in next dc, then 2 dc in 2nd dc.) Rpt to end of row—18 dc.

Rnd 4 (Work 2 dc in next dc, then 1 dc in next 2 dc.) Rpt to end of rnd—24 dc.

Rnds 5–7 Work 1 dc in each dc around.
Sl. st in next dc. Fasten off.

EYES (*make 2*)

Make as for 'red spots', using white yarn.

Pupils

Using black 8-ply yarn, work as for 'red spots' to rnd 2. Sl. st in next dc. Fasten off.

MOUTH

Upper Lip

With 3.25 mm knitting needles and red yarn, cast on 30 sts. Cast off.

Lower Lip

Work as for upper lip using 20 sts.

HUMPTY

TO MAKE UP

Legs

With right sides of one leg piece together sew sole and leg seam. Leave cast-off edge at top open. Turn to right side and fill firmly. With seam at centre back, sew top opening together. Complete other leg to match.

Arms

With right side of one arm piece together, sew arm and hand seam. Leave cast-off edge at top open. Turn to right side and fill firmly. With seam at underside, sew top opening together. Complete other arm to match.

Body

With right side of one body piece facing, pin each leg in position at bottom shapings, matching shaping edge to top edge of leg.
(Legs should lie facing inwards and on either side of the cast-on edge of the body piece.)
Pin the arms in position, approx. 25 mm above the legs, matching cast-off edges of arms to side edges of body pieces.
(*Ensure arms and legs all lie facing inwards.*)
With right sides together pin the other body piece over the top, matching shapings carefully (legs and arms will lie inside the two body pieces). Sew seam around the body catching in arms and legs as you go. Leave cast-off edges at top open. Turn to right side and fill body firmly. Sew cast-off edges at top together.

Collar and Bow Tie

Sew bow tie pieces to each end of the collar, ensuring they lie exactly in the centre.
Leaving a 1 cm gap at the front, sl. st the collar around the body. Position carefully so that the white section is to the bottom and just touches the arms. Tie bow tie in a neat bow.

Spots

Sl. st spots to the lower half of the body—7 on the front and 7 on the back.

Nose

Run a length of white yarn around the outer edge of the nose piece. Pull slightly and fill firmly. Cont. to pull the length of yarn till a ball is formed. Sl. st in position halfway between the top of collar and the top of head.

Mouth

Sl. st the mouth pieces in position as illustrated, curving the bottom lip and catching it under the upper lip at each end.

Eyes

Sl. st white eye sections to head and attach pupils over the top and slightly to one side as illustrated. Work a small backstitch in white yarn in centre of pupils. With a double strand of black 8-ply yarn embroider eyebrows as illustrated.

Hair

Cut 40 lengths of black 12-ply yarn approx. 15 cm long. Thread each strand through the top of the head, slightly to one side and so that they lie in a neat row from front to back. Backstitch in position, then run a double strand over the whole lot to form a part.

BANANA IN PYJAMAS AND BABY TEDDY BEAR

You won't be able to resist creating this favourite fellow, first seen on *Play School*. Banana in Pyjamas comes complete with a baby teddy bear so you can bring the song to life.

Banana in Pyjamas
and
Baby Teddy Bear **C

Description

Banana in Pyjamas

Trousers, body and arms are knitted in two identical pieces—one for the front and one for the back. Body of jacket is knitted in one piece and sleeves of jacket in one piece each. Collar is knitted up separately. Brown top on head is knitted in one piece. Base of legs are crocheted and mouth embroidered. When completed, he stands approx. 30 cm tall.

Baby Teddy Bear

Knitted in two identical pieces. Eyes, nose and mouth are embroidered. When completed, he stands approx. 10 cm tall.

Materials

Banana

One 50 g ball yellow 8-ply yarn
One 25 g ball blue 8-ply yarn
One 25 g ball white 8-ply yarn
Small quantities of brown and black 8-ply yarns
One pair 3.25 mm knitting needles
One 3.5 mm crochet hook
One pair 8 mm animal safety eyes
3 small white buttons
Tapestry needle
Polyester fibre filling

Teddy

One 20 g ball tan 8-ply yarn

Abbreviations

See page 4.

Banana in Pyjamas

Front

To Shape Trousers

With 3.25 mm knitting needles and blue yarn, cast on 30 sts.
K 1 row.
Join in white yarn and working in stripes of 2 rows white and 2 rows blue, knit a further 14 rows.
Cast off 18 sts at beg. of next row.
K 1 row.
Cast on 18 sts at beg. of next row.
Cont. to work in stripes of blue and white for a further 14 rows.
Cast off.

To Shape Body

With 3.25 mm knitting needles and yellow yarn pick up 17 sts across top of trousers (R.S. facing).
Commencing with a P row, work 9 rows st.st.

To Shape Arms

Cast on 12 sts at beg. of next 2 rows—41 sts.
Work 6 rows.
Cast off 12 sts at beg. of next 2 rows.
Cont. in st.st for a further 20 rows.

To Shape Head

Dec. at each end of every row till 3 sts rem.
P3 tog. Fasten off.

Back

Work as for front.

BANANA IN PYJAMAS

Base of Legs (make 2)

With 3.5 mm crochet hook and yellow yarn, make 2 ch.

Rnd 1 Work 6 dc in 2nd ch. from hook.

Rnd 2 Work 2 dc in each dc around—12 dc.

Rnd 3 (Work 1 dc in next dc then 2 dc in 2nd dc) Rpt to end of rnd—18 dc.
St.st in next dc. Fasten off.

Top of Banana

With 3.25 mm knitting needles and brown yarn, cast on 8 sts.
Work 6 rows st.st.
Break off yarn leaving a long length and thread through these 8 sts. Pull firmly and with right sides together sew side seam.

Jacket

With 3.25 mm knitting needles and blue yarn, cast on 20 sts.
Work in g. st stripes of 2 rows blue and 2 rows white, inc. at beg. of next and foll. alt. rows till 30 sts.
K 9 rows.

To Shape Armholes

K4. Cast off 10 sts. K to end.

Next row K16 sts, turn, cast on 10 sts, turn, K last 4 sts.
Cont. in stripe pattern for a further 46 rows.
Work another armhole as before.
K 10 rows.
Dec. at beg. of next and foll. alt. rows till 22 sts rem.
K 1 row.

To Work Buttonholes

K2 tog., K3, y. fwd, K2 tog., K4, y. fwd, K2 tog., K4, y. fwd, K2 tog., K3.
Cont. to dec. at beg. of alt. rows till 20 sts rem. Cast off.

Sleeves (make 2)

With 3.25 mm knitting needles and blue yarn, cast on 12 sts.
Work in g. st stripes of 2 rows blue and 2 rows white for 36 rows.
Cast off.

Collar

With 3.25 mm knitting needles, white yarn and with W.S. of jacket facing, pick up 50 sts evenly around neck edge.
K 1 row.
Join in blue yarn and work in stripes as before for a further 5 rows.
Cast off.

To Make Up

Body

Attach animal safety eyes to one body piece. Position carefully slightly below head shaping and equal distance from the side edges. With right sides together sew seam around body, arms and trousers, leaving base of legs and top of head shaping open. With right sides together sew base of legs to bottom of trouser legs. Turn to right side and fill firmly. Sew opening at top of head.

Top of Banana

Turn piece to right side and fill firmly. Slip stitch in position at top of head.

Jacket

Sew side seam of each sleeve and with right sides of sleeve and jacket together sew in position at each armhole.
Roll collar to right side and slip stitch in position.
Sew on buttons.

Embroider mouth in black yarn as illustrated.

BABY TEDDY BEAR

BABY TEDDY BEAR

With 3.25 mm knitting needles, tan yarn, and beg. with right leg, cast on 5 sts.
K 8 rows.
Break yarn and leave sts on needle. Work another leg the same. *Do not break yarn.*
K 2 rows across both legs—10 sts.
Inc. at each end of next row—12 sts.
K 9 rows.

To Shape Arms

Cast on 5 sts at beg. of next 2 rows—22 sts.
K 4 rows.
Cast off 7 sts at beg. of next 2 rows—8 sts.

To Shape Head

K 12 rows. Cast off.

TO MAKE UP

Place the two pieces together and sew around body and between legs. Leave cast-off edges at top of head open.
Turn to right side and fill loosely.
Sew seam across head.
Run a length of brown yarn around neck and pull firmly to shape.
Tie off.
Embroider eyes, nose, mouth and ears as illustrated.

Here's the song:

*Bananas
in Pyjamas
are coming down the stairs
Bananas
in Pyjamas
are coming down in pairs
Bananas
in Pyjamas
are chasing teddy bears
'cos on Tuesdays
they all try to
CATCH them unawares!*

Words of 'Bananas In Pyjamas' song by Carey Blyton, © 1972 Carey Blyton. Reprinted by permission of ABC Music Publishing. All rights reserved.

SLUSH

Slush pops up in all sorts of stories on *Play School*. Slush's pink spots and twirly tail are just what every pig would love to have.

DAISY

Daisy is *Play School*'s cow with a difference—she's purple! Every detail is knitted in this cute toy, even her udder.

SLUSH **

Description

Body is knitted in four pieces, one for each side, nose piece and mouth insert. Legs and ears are knitted in two pieces each and tail in one piece. Nostrils and patches on back are embroidered. When completed Slush stands approx. 17 cm high and is approx. 28 cm long.

Materials

One 100 g ball dark pink 8-ply yarn
Small quantities of burgundy, pale pink, black and tan 8-ply yarns
One pair 10 mm animal safety eyes
One pair 3.25 mm knitting needles
Tapestry needle
Polyester fibre filling

Abbreviations

See page 4.

Body—Left Side

With 3.25 mm knitting needles, dark pink yarn and beg. at rear end, cast on 16 sts.
Working in st.st inc. at each end of every row till 30 sts, then in foll. alt. rows till 40 sts.
Work 23 rows straight.
Dec. at each end of next and foll. alt. rows till 30 sts rem.
P 1 row.

To Shape Head

Row 1 Inc. in first st, K27, K2 tog.
Row 2 P.
Rpt last 2 rows twice.
Row 7 K to last 2 sts, K2 tog.—29 sts.
Row 8 P.
Row 9 K2 tog., K25, K2 tog.—27 sts.
Row 10 P.

To Shape Snout

Next row K2 tog., K17, turn (leave 8 sts).
Next row P to end.
Working on these last 18 sts only, dec. at beg. of next and foll. alt. rows 4 times. *At the same time*, inc. at each end of 3rd and foll. 4th row—16 sts.
P 1 row.
Next row K.
Next row P.
Next row K2 tog., K13, inc. in last st.
Next row P.
Rpt last 4 rows twice. Cast off.

To Shape Mouth

Ret. to rem. 8 sts.
Dec. at beg. of next and foll. alt. rows till 2 sts rem. P2 tog. Fasten off.

Body—Right Side

Work as for left side, reversing shaping.

Mouth Insert

With 3.25 mm knitting needles and burgundy yarn, cast on 6 sts.
St.st 24 rows.
Inc. at each end of next row—8 sts.
K 1 row.
Dec. at each end of next and foll. 4th rows till 2 sts rem. P2 tog. Fasten off.

Nose Piece

With 3.25 mm knitting needles and dark pink yarn, cast on 4 sts.
Working in st.st, inc. at each end of every row till 10 sts, then in alt. rows till 14 sts.
St.st 3 rows.
Dec. at each end of next and foll. alt. rows till 10 sts rem.
P 1 row.
Dec. at each end of every row till 4 sts rem. Cast off.

Legs (*make 8*)

With 3.25 mm knitting needles and

SLUSH

dark pink yarn, cast on 12 sts.
St.st 8 rows.

Next row K6, turn (leave 6 sts).

Next row P to end.
Working on these last 6 sts dec. at end of next and foll. alt. rows till 2 sts rem.
P2 tog. Fasten off.
Ret. to rem. 6 sts.
St.st 2 rows.
Dec. at beg. of next and foll. alt. rows till 2 sts rem.
P2 tog. Fasten off.

BACK EAR PIECE (make 2)

With 3.25 mm knitting needles and pale pink yarn, cast on 6 sts.

Next row Inc. K wise in every st—12 sts.
Working in g. st, inc. at each end of next 2 rows—16 sts.
K 9 rows.
Dec. at each end of next and foll. alt. rows till 6 sts rem.
Dec. at each end of foll. 4th rows till 2 sts rem.
K 1 row.
K2 tog. Fasten off.

FRONT EAR PIECE (make 2)

With 3.25 mm knitting needles and dark pink yarn, cast on 4 sts.

Next row Inc. K wise in every st—8 sts.
Working in st.st, beg. with a P row, inc. at each end of next 2 rows—12 sts.
St.st 5 rows.
Dec. at each end of every row till 6 sts rem., then at each end of alt. rows till 2 sts rem.
P 1 row.
K2 tog. Fasten off.

TAIL

With 3.25 mm knitting needles and dark pink yarn, cast on 40 sts loosely. Cast off firmly. Tail will fall into a curl.

TO MAKE UP

Body

Attach animal safety eyes to front head sections. Position carefully approx. 25 mm down from top edge and just beind mouth shapings. With right sides together sew one side of mouth insert to one side of body, matching long side to side of snout and pointed end to tip of mouth. (*Note* Long end of mouth insert forms underside of snout.) Sew other side of mouth insert to other body side to match. Body pieces should meet at tip of mouth.
With right sides together sew seam around the two body pieces, leaving cast-on edges at rear and cast-off edges at end of snout open. With right sides together, sew nose piece to end of snout, matching cast-off edge to top of snout and cast-on edge to end of mouth insert.
Turn to right side and fill firmly.
Sew cast-on edges at rear together.

Legs

With the right sides of two leg pieces together, sew down each side and between trotters. Leave cast-on edges open. Turn to right side and fill firmly. Complete other three legs to match. Sl. st in position to underside of body.

Ears

Matching cast-on edges, sl. st the wrong side of the front ear piece to the centre of the back ear piece. Ensure stitching does not go through to the back. Complete other ear to match, curving cast-on edges slightly. Sl. st to either side of the head as illustrated.

Tail

Sew one end of tail to the top of the rear seam.

With black yarn, satin stitch nostrils on lower half of nose piece.
With tan yarn, and working in satin stitch embroider patches on back as illustrated.

Daisy ***

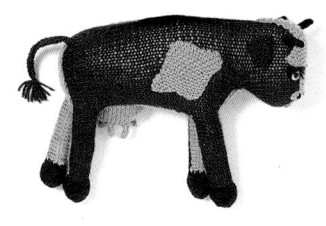

Description

Body, legs and head are knitted in three pieces—two side pieces and underside; hooves are knitted up separately. Ears, horns, udder, teats, tail and coloured patches are all knitted in one piece each. Nostrils, mouth and eye lashes are embroidered. When completed she stands approx. 18 cm high and is approx. 27 cm long.

Materials

One 50 g ball purple 8-ply yarn
One 25 g ball mauve 8-ply yarn
One 20 g ball black 8-ply yarn
One pair 10 mm 'sew-on' animal eyes
One pair 3.25 mm knitting needles
Tapestry needle
Polyester fibre filling

Abbreviations

See page 4.

Body—Right Side

With 3.25 mm knitting needles, purple yarn and beg. at hind leg, cast on 40 sts.
St.st 8 rows.
Cast off 20 sts at beg. of next row.
St.st 29 rows straight for body.

To Shape Front Leg

Cast on 20 sts at beg. of next row.
St.st 7 rows.
Cast off 20 sts at beg. of next row.
P 1 row.

To Shape Head

Dec. at beg. of next row and at this same edge on every foll. row till 13 sts rem.
St.st 3 rows.
Inc. at beg. of next row and at this same edge on every foll. row till 16 sts, then in alt. rows till 20 sts.
St.st 5 rows.
Dec. at beg. of next row and at this same edge on every foll. row till 16 sts rem. Cast off.

Body—Left Side

Work as for right side, reversing all shapings.

Underside

With 3.25 mm knitting needles, mauve yarn and beg. at rear end, cast on 2 sts.
Working in st.st, inc. at each end of 5th and foll. 6th rows till 10 sts.
St.st 3 rows.

To Shape Back Legs

*Cast on 20 sts at beg. of next 2 rows—50 sts.
St.st 6 rows.
Cast off 20 sts at beg. of next 2 rows—10 sts rem.**
St.st 28 rows straight for body.

To Shape Front Legs

Work as for back legs from * to **.

To Shape Head

Dec. at each end of next row—8 sts.
St.st 9 rows.
Dec. at each end of next row—6 sts.
St.st 15 rows.
Dec. at each end of next and foll. alt. rows till 2 sts rem.
P 1 row.
K2 tog. Fasten off.

Hooves

First, with right sides together join the two side pieces, sewing seam across cast-off edges at front, over head and along back. Sew underside piece in position from tip of nose, under head and down each front leg. Then, with right side facing and black yarn, pick up 14 sts evenly along the end of one front leg.
P 1 row.

27

Daisy

Next row Inc. in 1st st, K5, (inc. in next st) twice, K5, inc. in last st—18 sts.
St.st 5 rows.

Next row K2 tog. to end—9 sts.

Next row (P2 tog.) twice, P1, (P2 tog.) twice—5 sts.
Break off yarn leaving a long end, thread it through rem. 5 sts and pull firmly. Sew side seam of hoof. Work other front hoof to match. Cont. to sew seam down the back of each front leg, and along underside side of body. (*Note* Leave 10 cm open at one side.) Cont. to sew down the front of each back leg.
Work hooves as before, at the end of each back leg.
Complete seams at back of legs and body, matching cast-on edge of underside piece to back centre seam.
Turn to right side. Fill firmly and sew up opening.

Tail

With 3.25 mm knitting needles and purple yarn, cast on 4 sts.
St.st 30 rows. Break yarn, leaving a long end, thread it through these 4 sts, pull firmly and tie off.

Ears (*make 2*)

With 3.25 mm knitting needles and purple yarn, cast on 4 sts.

Next row Inc. in every st—8 sts.
K 1 row.
Inc. at each end of next row—10 sts.
K 3 rows.
Dec. at each end of next and foll. alt. rows till 2 sts rem.
K 1 row. K2 tog. Fasten off.

Horns (*make 2*)

With 3.25 mm knitting needles and black yarn, cast on 4 sts.
St.st 6 rows. Break off yarn leaving a long end, and thread it through these 4 sts. Pull firmly and tie off.

Udder

With 3.25 mm knitting needles and mauve yarn, cast on 32 sts.
St.st 4 rows.

Row 5 K2 tog., K12, K2 tog., K2 tog. t.b.l., K12, K2 tog. t.b.l.—28 sts.

Row 6 P2 tog. t.b.l., P10, P2 tog. t.b.l., P2 tog., P10, P2 tog—24 sts.

Row 7 K2 tog., K8, K2 tog., K2 tog. t.b.l., K8, K2 tog. t.b.l.—20 sts.

Row 8 P2 tog. t.b.l., P6, P2 tog. t.b.l., P2 tog., P6, P2 tog.—16 sts.

Row 9 K2 tog., K4, K2 tog., K2 tog. t.b.l., K4, K2 tog. t.b.l—12 sts.

Row 10 P2 tog. t.b.l., P2, P2 tog. t.b.l., P2 tog., P2, P2 tog.—8 sts.

Row 11 (K2 tog.) twice, (K2 tog. t.b.l.) twice—4 sts.
Break yarn leaving a long end and thread it through rem. 4 sts.
Pull firmly and tie off.

Teats (*make 4*)

With 3.25 mm knitting needles and mauve yarn, cast on 3 sts.
St.st 4 rows.
Break yarn leaving a long end, and thread it through these 4 sts.
Pull firmly and tie off.

... continued on page 76

FIDO **

Description

Body, legs and head are knitted in three pieces—two side pieces and underside. Ears are knitted in two pieces and tail, nose flaps and nose in one piece each. The harness is in three pieces. When completed he is approx. 35 cm long.

Fido is one of the dogs from *Play School* and comes complete with harness so you can take him for a walk. His floppy ears and knitted snout give him a lovingly loyal look.

Materials

One 100 g ball orange 8-ply yarn
One 50 g ball yellow 8-ply yarn
One 25 g ball choc. brown 8-ply yarn
Two brown buttons
One pair 3.25 mm knitting needles
Tapestry needle
Polyester fibre filling

Abbreviations

See page 4.

Body—Right Side

With 3.25 mm knitting needles, orange yarn and beg. at hind leg, cast on 40 sts.

To Shape Paw

*K4, turn.
Slip 1 P wise, P3.
K6, turn.
Slip 1 P wise, P5.
St.st 10 rows across all sts.
K6, turn.
Slip 1 P wise, P5.

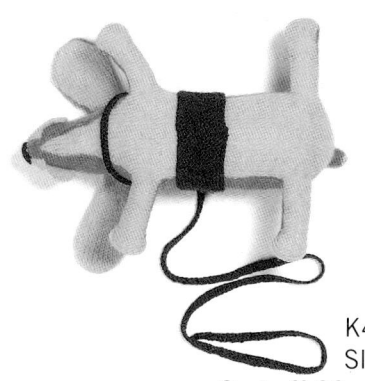

Fido

K4 turn.
Slip 1 P wise, P3.
Cast off 20 sts at the beg. of next row—20 sts rem.**
St.st 41 rows straight for the body.

To Shape Front Leg

Cast on 20 sts at beg. of row.
Rep. from * to ** once.
P 1 row.

To Shape Head

Next row K2 tog., K to last st, inc. in last st.

Next row P.
Rpt last two rows 4 times.

Next row K2 tog., K to end.

Next row P.
Rpt last two rows once—18 sts rem.

Next row K to the last 2 sts, K2 tog.

Next row P.
Rpt last two rows 5 times—
12 sts rem.

To Shape Nose

Dec. at each end of 3rd and foll. 4th rows till 6 sts rem.
P 1 row. Cast off.

Body—Left Side

Work as for right side, reversing all shaping.

Underside

With 3.25 mm knitting needles, yellow yarn and beg. at rear end, cast on 4 sts.
Working in st.st inc. at each end of 2nd and foll. 3rd rows till 20 sts.
P 1 row.

To Shape Back Legs

*Cast on 20 sts at beg. of row—
40 sts.
K4, turn.
Slip 1 P wise, P3.
K6, turn.
Slip 1 P wise, P5.
K to end of row.
Cast on 20 sts at beg. of row—
60 sts.
P4, turn.
Slip 1 K wise, K3.
P6, turn.
Slip 1 K wise, K5.
St.st 9 rows across all sts.
K6, turn.
Slip 1 P wise, P5.
K4, turn.
Slip 1 P wise, P3.
Cast off 20 sts at beg. of next row—
40 sts rem.
P6, turn.
Slip 1 K wise, K5.
P4, turn.
Slip 1 K wise, K 3.
Cast off 20 sts at beg. of next row—
20 sts rem.**
St.st 40 rows straight for body.

To Shape Front Legs

Work as back legs from * to **.
Dec. at each end of next and foll. alt. rows till 6 sts rem.
St.st 15 rows.
Dec. at each end of next and foll. 4th row—2 sts rem.
P 1 row.
K2 tog. Fasten off.

Ears (make 2 orange, 2 yellow)

With 3.25 mm knitting needles, cast on 10 sts.
St.st 10 rows.
Inc. at each end of next and foll. 6th rows till 18 sts.
St.st 3 rows.
Dec. at each end of next and foll. alt. rows till 10 sts rem.
Dec. at each end of every row till 4 sts rem. Cast off.

Tail

With 3.25 mm knitting needles and orange yarn, cast on 20 sts.

Next row K2 tog. across the row—
10 sts.
Beg. with a P row, st.st 9 rows.
Break off orange yarn and join in yellow yarn.
K 1 row.

FIDO

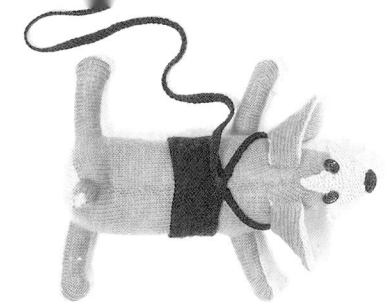

Next row P2 tog. across row—5 sts. Break off yarn leaving a long end, thread it through rem. 5 sts and pull firmly. Tie off.

NOSE FLAP

With 3.25 mm knitting needles and yellow yarn, cast on 18 sts.
Working in g. st inc. at each end of every row till 28 sts.
K 1 row.
Inc. at each end of next row—30 sts.
K 6 rows.
Dec. at each end of next row—28 sts.
K 1 row.
Dec. at each end of every row till 10 sts rem.
K 1 row.
Dec. at each end of next and foll. alt. rows till 6 sts rem., then at each end of foll. 6th rows till 2 sts rem.
K 1 row. Cast off.

NOSE PIECE

With 3.25 mm knitting needles and choc. brown yarn, cast on 2 sts.
Working in g. st inc. at each end of every row till 6 sts.
K 8 rows.
Dec. at each end of every row till 2 sts rem. Cast off.

HARNESS

With 3.25 mm knitting needles and choc. brown yarn, cast on 64 sts.
K 24 rows. Cast off.

Strap

Cast on 70 sts. K 1 row. Cast off.

Lead

Cast on 200 sts. K 1 row. Cast off.

TO MAKE UP

Body

With right sides of the two body pieces together, sew seam from top of nose, along head and back to cast-on edges at rear. Sew underside in position, matching cast-on edge to centre back seam and front point to under nose section. Match leg shapings carefully. Leave an opening approx. 10 cm at one side of body section. Sew seam under nose and thread a long piece of yarn around cast-off edges at end of nose. Pull firmly to close gap and tie off. Turn to right side and fill firmly. Sew up opening at underside.

Ears

With right sides of one orange and one yellow piece together, sew around ear shaping, leaving cast-on edges open. Turn to right side. (*Note* Ears are not filled). Oversew cast-on edges together and slip stitch this edge to top of head approx. 2 cm down from centre seam. Ensure orange side lies to the top. Complete other ear to match.

Tail

Fold in half lengthwise and sew side seam. Turn to right side and fill firmly. Sl. stitch in position at end of centre back seam.

Nose Flap

Sl. stitch cast-on edge across top of nose, and top shaped section down to each side of the head. Leave rounded flaps at each side loose, and just curve them slightly so they point outwards.

Nose Piece

Sl. stitch in position over the top of the nose section. Sew on buttons just above nose flaps as illustrated.

Harness

Join row ends at underside. Mark the exact centre of the cast-off edge and sew each end of strap at this point. Attach lead to harness just behind this point. Make a large loop at end of lead and sew in position. Slip harness over head and around body so that the strap lies in front of front legs and under chest.

McDuff ***c

Description
Body is knitted in five pieces. two face pieces, two rim pieces and one piece for the bellows. Mouth strap is knitted and nose, eyes and mouth screws are crocheted. When completed he stands approx. 32 cm high.

Materials
Two 100 g balls yellow 8-ply yarn
One 50 g ball blue 8-ply yarn
One 25 g ball black 8-ply yarn
Small quantities red, white and gold 8-ply yarns
One pair 3.25 mm knitting needles
One 3.5 mm crochet hook
Tapestry needle
Polyester fibre filling

Abbreviations
See page 4.

McDuff is a slightly off-key concertina. She is brave, timid and a little bit silly, all at the same time, and she's a most faithful friend.

McDUFF

Face Pieces (make 2)

With 3.25 mm knitting needles and blue yarn, cast on 120 sts.

Row 1 K8, sl. 1, K1, P.S.S.O., (K2 tog., K16, sl. 1, K1, P.S.S.O.) 5 times, K2 tog., K8.

Next and foll. alt. rows P.

Row 3 K7, sl. 1, K1, P.S.S.O., (K2 tog., K14, sl. 1, K1, P.S.S.O.) 5 times, K2 tog., K7.

Row 5 K6, sl. 1, K1, P.S.S.O., (K2 tog., K12, sl. 1, K1, P.S.S.O.) 5 times, K2 tog., K6.

Row 7 K5, sl. 1, K1, P.S.S.O., (K2 tog., K10, sl. 1, K1, P.S.S.O.) 5 times, K2 tog., K5.

Row 9 K4, sl. 1, K1, P.S.S.O., (K2 tog., K8, sl. 1, K1, P.S.S.O.) 5 times, K2 tog., K4.

Row 11 K3, sl. 1, K1, P.S.S.O., (K2 tog., K6, sl. 1, K1, P.S.S.O.) 5 times, K2 tog., K3.

Row 13 K2, sl. 1, K1, P.S.S.O., (K2 tog., K4, sl. 1, K1, P.S.S.O.) 5 times, K2 tog., K2.

Row 15 K1, sl. 1, K1, P.S.S.O., (K2 tog., K3, sl. 1, K1, P.S.S.O.) 5 times, K2 tog., K1.

Row 17 (sl. 1, K1, P.S.S.O., K2 tog.) to end—12 sts.

Row 18 P.

Break yarn leaving a long end. Thread it through these 12 sts and pull firmly. Tie off.

Bellows

With 3.25 mm knitting needles and yellow yarn, work as for face piece till Row 10 has been completed—60 sts.

Row 11 K.

Next and foll. alt. rows P.

Row 13 K5, m.2, (K10, m.2) to last 5 sts. K5.

Row 15 K6, m.2, (K12, m.2) to last 6 sts. K6.

Row 17 K7, m.2, (K14, m.2) to last 7 sts. K7.

Row 19 K8, m.2, (K16, m.2) to last 8 sts. K8.

Row 21 K9, m.2, (K18, m.2) to last 9 sts. K9.

Row 22 P 120 sts.

Rpt rows 1–22 four times. Cast off.

Rim Pieces (make 2)

With 3.25 mm knitting needles and black yarn, cast on 120 sts. Beg. with a K row, st.st 6 rows. Cast off.

Mouth Strap

With 3.25 mm knitting needles and red yarn, cast on 5 sts. K 60 rows. Cast off.

Nose

With 3.5 mm crochet hook and black yarn, make 2 ch.

Rnd 1 Work 6 dc in 2nd ch. from hook.

Rnd 2 Work 2 dc in each dc around—12 dc.

Rnd 3 (Work 1 dc in next dc then 2 dc in 2nd dc.) Rpt to end of rnd—18 dc.

Sl. st in next dc. Fasten off.

Eyes (make 2)

Work as for nose till Rnd 2 has been completed. Break off black yarn and join in white yarn. Complete as for nose.

Mouth Screws (make 2)

With 3.5 mm crochet hook and gold yarn, make 2 ch. Work 6 dc in 2nd ch. from hook. Sl. st in next dc. Fasten off.

McDUFF

TO MAKE UP

Face Pieces

Fold right sides of one piece together and sew seam from centre to cast-on edge. Complete other face piece to match.

Rim Pieces

Fold right sides of one piece together and sew seam across side edge, forming a large loop. Complete other edge piece to match.

Bellows

Fold right sides together lengthwise and sew back seam from cast-on edge to cast-off edge. Match shaping carefully. Turn to right side.
With wrong sides together and matching back seams, sew cast-on edge of one rim piece around cast-on edge of one face piece. Sew cast-on edge of bellows piece to cast-off edge of this rim piece in the same way. Sew other rim piece to end of bellows piece. Fill loosely, carefully pushing filling into corners as you go. Matching back seam and corners, sew remaining face piece around rim piece.
Sl. st ends of mouth strap, mouth screws, nose and eyes in position, as illustrated. Following the two front lines of shaping, run lengths of yarn through the bellows from top to bottom and pull slightly to bend face forward. Tie off securely.

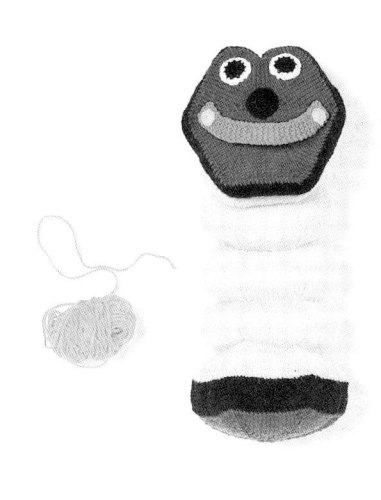

stocking stitch

garter stitch

JOHNSON

Johnson leads the other toys—he's trusting, generous and a true friend. He will become a favourite bedroom mate.

JOHNSON ***C

DESCRIPTION

Back is knitted in one piece. Front including trunk is knitted in two pieces. Arms are knitted separately in one piece each, ears in two pieces each and eye ridges in one piece each. Base of legs, arms and trunk are crocheted. When completed he stands approx. 38 cm tall.

MATERIALS

Three 50 g balls pink 8-ply yarn (Mohair may also be used.)
One 50 g ball pale grey 8-ply yarn
Small quantity white 8-ply yarn
One pair 18 mm black animal safety eyes
One pair 3.25 mm knitting needles
One 3.5 mm crochet hook
Tapestry needle
Polyester fibre filling

ABBREVIATIONS

See page 4.

BACK

With 3.25 mm knitting needles, pink yarn and beg. with left leg, cast on 15 sts.
K 30 rows.
Break yarn and leave on needle.
Work another leg the same. *Do not break yarn.*
K 2 rows across both legs—30 sts.
Next row Inc. in every st—60 sts*.
K 25 rows.
Dec. at each end of next and foll. alt. rows till 20 sts rem. K 1 row.

To Shape Head

Inc. at each end of next and foll. alt. rows till 30 sts.
K 31 rows. Cast off.

FRONT

Work as for back to *.
K 19 rows.

To Shape Stomach Patch

Row 1 K25 sts pink, join in grey yarn, K10 sts, join in pink yarn, K25 sts.
(*See* 'Useful Information' on page 5 for changing colours in the middle of a row.)

Row 2 K24 pink, K12 grey, K24 pink.

Rows 3 & 4 K23 pink, K14 grey, K23 pink.

Rows 5 & 6 K22 pink, K16 grey, K22 pink.

Row 7 K2 tog., K19 pink, K18 grey, K19, K2 tog. pink.

Next and foll. alt. rows K pink sts pink, and grey sts grey, as they appear.

Row 9 (K2 tog., K17) pink, K20 grey, (K17, K2 tog.) pink.

Row 11 (K2 tog., K15) pink, K22 grey, (K15, K2 tog.) pink.

Row 13 (K2 tog., K13) pink, K24 grey, (K13, K2 tog.) pink.

Row 15 (K2 tog., K12) pink, K24 grey, (K12, K2 tog.) pink.

Row 17 (K2 tog., K11) pink, K24 grey, (K11, K2 tog.) pink.

Row 19 (K2 tog., K10) pink, K24 grey, (K10, K2 tog.) pink.

Row 21 (K2 tog., K10) pink, K22 grey, (K10, K2 tog.) pink.
Cont. to work in this way, dec. at each end of alt. rows and working one less st at each end of grey area till only 2 grey sts are left.
(*Note* There should always be 11 pink sts at each end of needle.)
Break off grey yarn and second ball of pink yarn.
Cont. to dec. at each end of alt. rows till 20 sts rem.
K 1 row.

JOHNSON

To Shape Underside of Trunk

Inc. at each end of next and foll. alt. rows till 30 sts.
K 1 row.
Place markers of coloured yarn at each end of last row.
Dec. at each end of next and foll. alt. rows till 14 sts rem.
K 13 rows.
Dec. at each end of next and foll. 14th rows till 8 sts rem.
K 13 rows. Cast off.

TRUNK AND FACE

With 3.25 mm knitting needles, pink yarn and beg. with end of trunk, cast on 8 sts.
K 14 rows.
Inc. at each end of next and foll. 14th rows till 14 sts.
K 13 rows.
Inc. at each end of next and foll. alt. rows till 30 sts.
K 1 row.
Place markers of coloured yarn at each end of last row.
K 4 rows.

To Shape Eyes

Row 1 K6 sts pink yarn, join in white yarn, K4, join in pink yarn, K10, join in white yarn, K4, join in pink yarn, K6.

Next and foll. alt. rows K colours as they appear.

Row 3 K4 pink, K8 white, K6 pink, K8 white, K45 pink.

Row 5 K5 pink, K6 white, K8 pink, K6 white, K5 pink.

Row 7 K6 pink, K4 white, K10 pink, K4 white, K6 pink.

Row 8 K colours as they appear. Cont. in pink only, breaking off all other yarns.
K 18 rows.
Cast off.

ARMS (make 2)

With 3.25 mm knitting needles and pink yarn, cast on 24 sts.
K 30 rows.

To Shape Armholes

Cast off 4 sts at beg. of next 2 rows—16 sts.
Dec. at each end of next and foll. alt. rows till 2 sts rem.
K2 tog. Fasten off.

EARS

Back

With 3.25 mm knitting needles and pink yarn, cast on 34 sts.
K 10 rows.
Dec. at beg. of next and foll. alt. rows till 30 sts rem.
K 1 row.
Cast off 12 sts at beg. of next row.
K 1 row.
Dec. at beg. of next and foll. alt. rows till 10 sts rem.
K 1 row.
Dec. at each end of every row till 2 sts rem.
K2 tog. Fasten off.
Work another piece the same, reversing shaping.

Front

With 3.25 mm knitting needles, cast on 3 sts pink, 28 sts grey and 3 sts pink—34 sts.
Working colours as they appear, K 10 rows.

To Work Shaping

Row 1 (K2 tog., K2) pink, K27 grey, K3 pink.

Next and foll. alt. rows Work colours as they appear.

Row 3 (K2 tog., K2) pink, K26 grey, K3 pink.

Row 5 (K2 tog., K13) pink, K14 grey, K3 pink.

Row 7 (K2 tog., K13) pink, K13 grey, K3 pink.

Row 9 Cast off 12 sts, K3 pink, K12 grey, K3 pink.

Row 10 K colours as they appear. Dec. at beg. of next and foll. alt. rows till 11 sts rem. *At the same*

JOHNSON

time, work one less st at beg. of grey area on next and foll. alt. rows. (*Note* There should always be 3 pink sts at each end of needle.
K 1 row.
Cont. in pink yarn only, K2 rows. Dec. at each end of every row till 2 sts rem.
K2 tog. Fasten off.
Work another piece the same, reversing shaping.

EYE RIDGES (*make 2*)

With 3.25 mm knitting needles and pink yarn, cast on 18 sts.
K 2 rows. Cast off.

BASE OF LEGS (*make 2*)

With 3.5 mm crochet hook and grey yarn, make 2 ch.

Rnd 1 Work 6 dc in 2nd ch. from hook.

Rnd 2 Work 2 dc in each dc around—12 dc.

Rnd 3 (Work 1 dc in next dc then 2 dc in 2nd dc.) Rpt to end of rnd—18 dc.

Rnd 4 (Work 2 dc in next dc then 1 dc in next 2 dc.) Rpt to end of rnd—24 dc.

Rnd 5 (Work 1 dc in next 3 dc then 2 dc in next dc.) Rpt to end of rnd—30 dc.
Sl. st in next dc. Fasten off.

BASE OF ARMS (*make 2*)

Work as for base of legs till rnd 4 has been completed.
Sl. st in next dc. Fasten off.

BASE OF TRUNK

Work as for base of legs till rnd 3 has been completed.
Sl. st in next dc. Fasten off.

TO MAKE UP

Trunk and Body

Attach animal safety eyes at the centre of the white sections on face piece.
With right sides of the two trunk pieces together, sew side seams from end of trunk to markers, matching shaping carefully.
Sew base of trunk in position.
With right sides of the two body pieces together (trunk should be to the inside) sew seams approx. 3 cm across top outside corner of head and down sides of head, body and legs. Sew between legs. Leave base of legs and small section at top of head open. With right sides together sew base of legs around each leg opening. Turn to right side and fill firmly. Sew up opening across top of head. Catch trunk down at centre neck.

Arms

Fold one arm piece in half lengthwise and sew side seam from cast-on edge to armhole shaping. Attach base of arm as for legs. Turn to right side and fill firmly. With top of armhole at neck edge, slip stitch armhole to side of body, and catch down to side at wrist. Complete other arm to match.

Ears

With right sides of one back piece and matching front piece together, sew seam around top, sides, bottom and along cast-on edges for a distance of approx. 4 cm. Leave remaining cast-on edges open. Turn to right side and fill loosely. Slip stitch cast-on edges to side of head, positioning carefully to either side of the side head seam. Complete other ear to match.

Eye Ridges

Position carefully over the top of each eye and slip stitch down at side edges and across top.

ALFRED

Alfred is a leaky hot water bottle which lives under Michael's bed. He can be a cantankerous old bully sometimes but still finds the other toys a lot of fun. Here, you can make him as a hand puppet.

40

ALFRED

Description

Front and back are knitted in one piece each. Hand inserts are knitted in two pieces. Plug and handle are knitted in one piece each. Pattern on front and back and letter 'A' are embroidered. Eyes are glued. When completed he measures approx. 20 cm x 30 cm.

Materials

Two 100 g balls green 8-ply yarn
Small quantities black and orange 8-ply yarns
One pair 3.25 mm knitting needles
One pair 20 mm oval 'stick-on' animal eyes
Craft glue
Tapestry needle
0.5 sq m thin wadding
Polyester fibre filling

Abbreviations

See page 4.

Front

With 3.25 mm knitting needles and green yarn cast on 46 sts. Place markers of coloured wool 11 sts in from each end for hand inserts.
K 4 rows.

Next row K3, P40, K3.

Next row K.
Rpt last two rows 34 times.

Neck Pattern

Row 1 K3, P19, K2, P19, K3.

Rows 2 and 4 K.

Row 3 K3, P17, K6, P17, K3.

Row 5 K3, P15, K10, P15, K3.
K 4 rows.
Cast off 17 sts at beg. of next 2 rows—12 sts rem.
K 6 rows.

To Shape Spout

Next row (Inc. in next st, K1) 3 times, (K1, inc. in next st) 3 times—18 sts.
Working in g. st, inc. at each end of every row till 32 sts.*
Cast off.

41

Alfred

Back

Work as for front to *.
K 1 row.

Next row (K2 tog.) twice, K to last 4 sts, (K2 tog.) twice.
Rpt last row till 8 sts rem.
Working in g. st dec. at each end of 6th row—6 sts rem.
K 1 row.
Dec. at each end of every row till 2 sts rem.
K2 tog. Fasten off.

Hand Inserts (*make 2*)

With 3.25 mm knitting needles and green yarn, cast on 24 sts.
K 40 rows.
Cont. in g. st, inc. at each end of next and foll. 4th rows till 36 sts.
K 3 rows.

*__Next row__ K10. Turn.
K to end.
Working on these first 10 sts only, dec. at each end of next and foll. alt. rows till 2 sts rem. K2 tog.
Fasten off.**
Join yarn to rem. 26 sts.

Next row K16. Turn.
Working on these first 16 sts only, inc. at each end of next and foll. alt. rows till 22 sts.
K 15 rows.
Dec. at each end of every row till 2 sts rem. K2 tog. Fasten off.
Join yarn to rem. 10 sts and complete to correspond with other side from * to **.

Plug

With 3.25 mm knitting needles and black yarn, cast on 12 sts.
Inc. K wise in every st—24 sts.
K 3 rows.

Next row (K4, K2 tog.) to end.

Next and alt. rows K.

Next row (K3, K2 tog.) to end.

Next row (K2, K2 tog.) to end.

Next row (K1, K2 tog.) to end.

Next row (K2 tog.) to end—4 sts.
Break yarn leaving a long end.
Thread it through rem. 4 sts, pull firmly and tie off.

Handle

With 3.25 mm knitting needles and orange yarn, cast on 4 sts.
St.st 12 rows. Cast off.

Alfred

To Make Up

Cut 2 pieces of wadding, the same size as front and back sections to beg. of neck shaping. Tack one piece of wadding to the wrong side of the front section around outer edge. Using green yarn and a long backstitch embroider star pattern as illustrated, catching in the wadding as you go. (*Note* It may be easier to draw the pattern on the knitted piece first using tailor's chalk.) Remove tacking stitches. Complete back to match.

Place the right sides of the two pieces together and sew seams from outer edges of spout down neck, across shoulders, down sides and across bottom edge to markers. Leave space between markers and top of spout open. Turn to right side. With the right sides together, sew cast-on edge of one hand insert to cast-on edge of front piece between markers. Sew other hand insert to back piece in the same way. Bring the two hand inserts together and sew seam around. Push the hand insert up between the two pieces of wadding, turning outside in as you go.

Plug

Fold right sides together and sew seam from centre to cast-on edge. Turn to right side and fill firmly. Slip stitch cast-on edge around inside edge of neck.

Handle

Fold wrong sides together lengthwise and sew side seam. Attach each end to either side of plug as illustrated.

Using green yarn and a fine backstitch embroider around g. st border, bringing front to back firmly. Work front and back hand inserts, and front and back neck shapings keeping front separate from back. With black yarn used double, embroider 'A' on front neck shaping as illustrated.

Glue eyes in position as illustrated.

RAGGY DOLLS

The Raggy Dolls live in the Reject bin in Mr Grime's toy factory, and when he isn't looking they climb out and have exciting adventures together. Princess, Sad Sack and Back-to-front are three of the dolls in the *Raggy Dolls* program.

THE RAGGY DOLLS

Sad Sack *c

Description

Legs, body and head are knitted in two pieces. one for the front and one for the back. Arms and nose are knitted in one piece each, the bow tie in two pieces and the hair in two pieces. Cheeks are crocheted. Eyes, eyebrows and mouth are embroidered. When completed he stands approx. 35 cm tall.

Materials

One 100 g ball yellow 8-ply yarn
One 25 g ball brown 5-ply yarn
One 25 g ball white 8-ply yarn
Small quantities crimson, black and red 8-ply yarns
One pair 3.25 mm knitting needles
One pair 3.00 mm knitting needles
One 3.5 mm crochet hook
Three large yellow buttons
Tapestry needle
Polyester fibre filling

Abbreviations

See page 4.

Sad Sack's plump round body used up too much stuffing so no-one wanted him. You'll find him very cute and cuddly, once you've knitted him yourself.

Sad Sack

Body—Front

With 3.25 mm knitting needles, yellow yarn, and beg. with the right foot, cast on 15 sts.
K, inc. in every st—30 sts.
K 14 rows.
K2 tog. across row—15 sts.
*K 20 rows.
Break off yarn and leave sts on needle. Work another leg the same. *Do not break yarn.*
Next row K1, (inc. in next st, K2) across both legs to the last 2 sts, inc. in next st, K1—40 sts.
K 41 rows.
Dec. at each end of next and foll. alt. rows till 30 sts rem.
K 1 row.
Dec. at each end of every row till 18 sts rem.

To Shape Head
Inc. at each end of next and foll. alt. rows till 24 sts.
K 23 rows.
Dec. at each end of next and foll. alt. rows till 16 sts rem.
K 1 row. Cast off.

Body—Back

With 3.25 mm knitting needles, yellow yarn and beg. with left foot, cast on 15 sts.
K1, (inc. in next st, K1) to end—22 sts.
K 14 rows.
K1, (K2 tog., K1) to end—15 sts.
Complete as for front from *.

Arms (make 2)

With 3.25 mm knitting needles, yellow yarn and beg. with the end of hand, cast on 8 sts.
Inc. in every st—16 sts.
Rpt this row once—32 sts.
K 8 rows.

Next row (K2 tog.) 3 times, K20, (K2 tog.) 3 times—26 sts.
K 7 rows.

Next row K3, (K2 tog., K2) twice, (K2 tog.) twice, (K2, K2 tog.) twice, K3—20 sts.
K 25 rows.

To Shape Armholes
Cast off 3 sts at beg. of next 2 rows—14 sts.
Dec. at each end of next and every foll. alt. row till 2 sts rem.
K 1 row.
K2 tog. Fasten off.

Nose

With 3.25 mm knitting needles, and yellow yarn, cast on 8 sts.
Inc. in every st—16 sts.
K 9 rows.
K2 tog. across row—8 sts.
Break yarn leaving a long end. Thread it through these 8 sts and pull firmly. Tie off.

Hair (make 2)

With 3.00 mm needles and brown 5-ply yarn, cast on 6 sts.
K 8 rows.
*Cast off 3 sts at beg of row, K to end of row.
K 1 row.
Cast on 3 sts at beg. of row, K to end of row.
K 7 rows.**
Rpt from * to ** 10 times. Cast off.

Bow Tie

To Make the Bow Piece
With 3.25 mm knitting needles and white yarn, cast on 10 sts.
K 80 rows. Cast off.

To Make the Tie Piece
Cast on 4 sts. K 20 rows. Cast off.

Cheeks (make 2)

With 3.5 mm crochet hook and crimson yarn, make 2 ch.
Rnd 1 Work 6 dc in 2nd ch. from hook.

Sad Sack

Rnd 2 Work 2 dc in each dc around—12 dc.

Rnd 3 (Work 1 dc in 1st dc, then 2 dc in 2nd dc.) Rpt to end of rnd—18 dc.
Sl. st in next dc. Fasten off.

To make up

Body

With right sides together, sew seam down each side of the head, body and legs, sew inner leg seams. Leave top of head open. Bring the cast-on edges of one foot together, so that the side seams meet. Sew along length of foot. Complete other foot to match. Turn to right side and fill firmly.
Sew seam at top of head.

Arms

Fold one arm in half lengthwise with right sides together and sew seam from armhole shaping, down arm and across cast-on edge. Turn to right side and fill firmly. Slip stitch armhole in place so that the top point lies just below neck shaping. Complete other arm to match. Slip stitch arms to body from armholes to wrists.

Nose

Sew seam from centre to cast-on edge. Turn to right side and fill firmly.
Slip stitch cast-on edge to face slightly below centre line.

Hair

Place the right sides of the two pieces together matching shapings carefully.
Sew seam around each ridge, leaving straight edges open.
Turn to right side, carefully pulling out each corner with a needle.
Placing the centre ridge at the exact centre of the head, slip stitch the front straight edge slightly forward of the seam line, and the back straight edge slightly behind the seam line.

Bow Tie

With double strands of red yarn and using a running stitch, work spots evenly along length of bow piece as illustrated. Complete tie pieces to match. With right sides of the bow piece together, fold cast-on and cast-off edges to the centre, sew seams across top and bottom edges. Turn to right side and sew cast-on and cast-off edges together. Wrap a length of yarn around the centre and pull firmly to gather. Tie off securely. Position the tie piece around the centre of the bow piece and sew cast-off and cast-on edges together. Slip stitch in position slightly below neck shaping.

Slip stitch cheeks in position.
With black yarn, embroider eyes in satin stitch and eyebrows and mouth in backstitch as illustrated.
Sew on buttons.

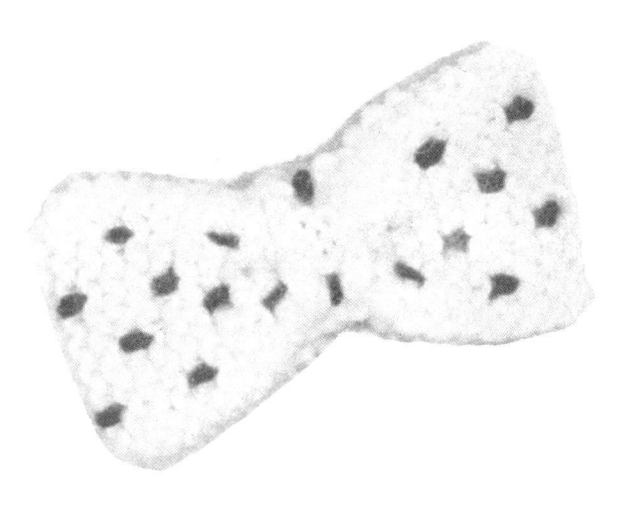

Princess

Princess should have had a tiara, beautiful hair and a splendid dress—but the machine dressed her in rags and cropped her hair by mistake. She's a rag doll with a difference!

PRINCESS **

DESCRIPTION

Legs, body and head are knitted in two pieces, one for the front and one for the back. Shoes, arms and nose are knitted in one piece each, and dress in two pieces. Eyes, cheeks and mouth are embroidered.
When completed she stands approx. 32 cm tall.

MATERIALS

One 50 g ball pink 8-ply yarn
One 25 g ball white 8-ply yarn
One 25 g ball crimson 8-ply yarn
One 25 g ball yellow 8-ply yarn
One 20 g ball bone 8-ply yarn
One 25 g ball yellow 12-ply yarn
Small quantities choc. brown, green, blue and turquoise 8-ply yarns
One pair 3.25 mm knitting needles
Three small crimson buttons
Tapestry needle
Polyester fibre filling

ABBREVIATIONS

See page 4.

BODY (make 2)

With 3.25 mm knittings needles, crimson yarn and beg. with right leg, cast on 8 sts.
St.st 4 rows.
Break off crimson yarn and join in white yarn.
St.st 4 rows.
Break off white yarn and join in choc. brown yarn.
St.st 4 rows.
Break off choc. brown yarn and join in pink yarn.
St.st 20 rows.
Break yarn and leave sts on needle. Work another leg the same. *Do not break yarn.*

To Shape Body

Next row (Inc. in 1st st, K6, inc. in next st.) Rpt across 2nd leg—20 sts.
St.st 25 rows.
Cast off 3 sts at beg. of next 4 rows—8 sts.
St.st 4 rows.

To Shape Head

Next row Inc. in every st—16 sts.
P 1 row.
Inc. at each end of next and foll. alt. row—20 sts.
St.st 15 rows.
Dec. at each end of next and foll. alt. row—16 sts.
P 1 row.
K2 tog. across row—8 sts.
Cast off P wise.

SHOES (make 2)

With 3.25 mm knitting needles and white yarn, cast on 8 sts.
Working in st.st inc. at each end of 7th and foll. 8th row—12 sts.
St.st 5 rows.
Dec. at each end of next and foll. 8th row—8 sts.
St.st 5 rows. Cast off.

ARMS (make 2)

With 3.25 mm knitting needles, pink yarn and beg. at end of hand, cast on 7 sts.
Inc. K wise in every st—14 sts.
Inc. P wise in every st—28 sts.
St.st 4 rows.

Next row (K2 tog.) 3 times, K16, (K2 tog.) 3 times—22 sts.
St.st 3 rows.

Next row K3, (K2 tog.) 8 times, K3—14 sts.
St.st 21 rows. Cast off.

Princess

Nose

With 3.25 mm knitting needles, and pink yarn, cast on 6 sts.
Inc. K wise in every st—12 sts.
St.st 5 rows.
K2 tog. across row—6 sts.
Break yarn leaving a long end.
Thread it through these 6 sts and pull firmly. Tie off.

Dress—Front

With 3.25 mm knitting needles and beg. at hem, cast on 6 sts in yellow yarn, 12 sts white yarn, 12 sts crimson yarn, 12 sts bone yarn, and 6 sts yellow yarn—48 sts.
W.S. facing.
Keeping colours correct, K 21 rows. (*See* 'Useful Information' on page 5 for changing colours in the middle of a row.)
Change crimson yarn for white yarn, and white yarn for crimson yarn.*
Cont., keeping colours correct, for a further 22 rows.
Break off all colours except the first yellow section.

To Shape Waistband

Next row K3 tog., (K2 tog.) 9 times, (K3 tog.) twice, (K2 tog.) 9 times, K3 tog.—22 sts.
K 3 rows.
Break off yellow yarn and join in crimson yarn for bodice.

To Shape Bodice

Inc. at each end of next and foll. alt. row—26 sts.
K 5 rows.

To Shape Armhole

Cast off 3 sts at the beg. of next 2 rows—20 sts.
K 4 rows.

Divide for Neck

K10, turn.
K to end.
Working on these last 10 sts, dec. at end of next and foll. alt. rows till 6 sts rem.
K 1 row.
Cast off 3 sts at beg. of next and foll. alt. row.
Ret. to rem. sts and complete other side to correspond, reversing shapings.

Dress—Back

Work as for front to *.

Divide for Back Opening

Next row Keeping colours correct, K24, turn.
Working on these 24 sts, complete skirt as for front to waistband.

To Shape Waistband

Next row K2 tog. across row—12 sts.
K 1 row.

Buttonhole row K to the last 3 sts, y. fwd, K2 tog., K1.
K 1 row.
Break off yellow yarn and join in crimson yarn for bodice.

To Shape Bodice

Inc. at the beg. of the next and foll. alt. row—14 sts.
K 5 rows.

To Shape Armhole

Cast of 3 sts at beg. of next row—11 sts.
K 5 rows.

Buttonhole row K to last 3 sts, y. fwd, K2 tog., K1.
K 9 rows.
Cast off 3 sts at beg. of next row—8 sts.
K 1 row.

Buttonhole row Cast off 3 sts, K to last 3 sts, y. fwd, K2 tog., K1—5 sts.
K 1 row. Cast off.

Complete other side to match, reversing shaping and omitting buttonholes.

PRINCESS

To Make Up

Body

With right sides of the two body pieces together, sew seam down each side of the head, body and legs. Sew inner leg seams. Leave top of head and base of legs open. Turn to right side and fill firmly. With a fine running st sew across top of legs bringing front to back—this will keep the legs movable. Sew seam across top of head.

Shoes

Fold one shoe in half with right sides together, bringing cast-on and cast-off edges together. Sew side seams. Turn to right side and fill firmly. Sew cast-on and cast-off edges together. Sl. st base of leg to top side of shoe. Position carefully so that the back of the leg is in line with the back of the shoe and the shoe will point slightly outwards. Complete other shoe to match.

Arms

Fold one arm in half lengthwise with right sides together and sew side seam and across cast-on edge. Turn to right side and fill firmly. With seam at centre underside, sew across cast-off edge. Sew this edge to side of body at beg. of shoulder shaping. Complete other arm to match.

Run lengths of yarn around waist, top of neck and wrists, pull firmly to shape and tie off securely.

Nose

Fold in half with right sides together and sew side seam. Leave cast-on edge open. Turn to right side and fill firmly. Sl. st cast-on edge to centre of face.

Dress

With right sides together, join shoulders and side seams. Turn to right side and using a long stitch embroider patterns on skirt as illustrated. Sew on buttons.

Hair

Using 12-ply yellow yarn make a fringe by sewing long loops through seam line at top of head, backstitching each loop as you go. Trim to length. Work around back of head in a similar fashion, making longer loops. Trim to length. Make a short tuft approx. I cm back from fringe. Thread lengths of yarn through centre stitch line from fringe to tuft. Backstitch securely.

Face

Embroider eyes in satin stitch, mouth in backstitch and cheeks by following the stitch lines as illustrated.

BACK-TO-FRONT

Back-to-front is a handyman doll with his own tool kit, but his head went on the wrong way round so he's never sure which way to go. Knit him up and join in his adventures.

BACK-TO-FRONT

Description

Legs, body and head are knitted in two pieces, one for the front and one for the back. Shoes, arms, nose and hat are knitted in one piece each and overalls in two pieces. Patch and pocket are knitted separately. Eyes, cheeks and mouth are embroidered. When completed he stands approx. 33 cm tall.

Materials

One 25 g ball pink 8-ply yarn
One 25 g ball lemon 8-ply yarn
One 25 g ball turquoise 8-ply yarn
One 25 g ball red 8-ply yarn
One 25 g ball white 8-ply yarn
One 25 g ball yellow 12-ply yarn
Small quantities aqua, blue, black and crimson 8-ply yarns
One pair 3.25 mm knitting needles
Tapestry needle
Polyester fibre filling

Abbreviations

See page 4.

Body (*make 2*)

With 3.25 mm knitting needles, pink yarn and beg. with right leg, cast on 8 sts.
St.st 32 rows.
Break yarn and leave sts on needle. Work another leg the same. *Do not break yarn.*

To Shape Body

Next row (Inc. in 1st st, K6, inc. in next st.) Rpt across 2nd leg—20 sts.
St.st 11 rows.
Break off pink yarn and join in lemon yarn for jumper.
St.st 14 rows.

To Shape Shoulder

Cast off 3 sts at beg. of next 4 rows—8 sts.
K 4 rows.
Break off lemon yarn and join in pink yarn for head.

To Shape Head

Next row Inc. in every st—16 sts.
P 1 row.
Inc. at each end of next row—18 sts.
St.st 21 rows.
Dec. at each end of next row—16 sts.
P 1 row.
K2 tog. across row—8 sts
Cast off P wise.

Shoes (*make 2*)

With 3.25 mm knitting needles and white yarn, cast on 8 sts.
Working in st.st inc. at each end of 7th and foll. 8th row—12 sts.
St.st 5 rows.
Dec. at each end of next and foll. 8th row—8 sts.
St.st 5 rows,. Cast off.

Arms (*make 2*)

With 3.25 mm knitting needles, white yarn and beg. at end of hand, cast on 7 sts.
Inc. K wise in every st—14 sts.
Inc. P wise in every st—28 sts.
St.st 4 rows.

Next row (K2 tog.) 3 times, K16, (K2 tog.) 3 times—22 sts.
St.st 3 rows.
Break off white yarn and join in lemon yarn for sleeves.

Next row K3, (K2 tog.) 8 times, K3—14 sts.
K 3 rows.
Beg. with a K row, st.st 20 rows.
Cast off.

BACK-TO-FRONT

Nose

With 3.25 mm knitting needles and pink yarn, cast on 6 sts.
Inc. K wise in every st—12 sts.
St.st 5 rows.
K2 tog. across row—6 sts. Break yarn leaving a long end. Thread it through these 6 sts and pull firmly. Tie off.

Overalls (make 2)

With 3.25 mm knitting needles, aqua yarn and beg. with right cuff, cast on 12 sts.
K 5 rows.
Break off aqua yarn and join in turquoise yarn for leg.
St.st 30 rows.
Break off yarn and leave sts on R.H. needle. Work another leg the same. *Do not break yarn.*
St.st 17 rows across both legs—24 sts.

Next row K5, P14, K5.

To Shape Bib

Cast off 5 sts, K13 turn. Cont. to work on these 14 sts only.

Next row K1, P12, K1.

Next row K.
Rpt last 2 rows 5 times.
K 1 row. Cast off.
Ret. to rem. 5 sts. Cast off.

Straps (make 2)

With 3.25 mm knitting needles and turquoise yarn, cast on 10 sts.
Cast off.

Pocket

With 3.25 mm knitting needles and turquoise yarn, cast on 2 sts.
Working in st.st, inc. at each end of every row till 10 sts.
St.st 7 rows. Cast off K wise.

Patch

With 3.25 mm knitting needles and red yarn, cast on 8 sts.
K 12 rows. Cast off.

Hat

With 3.25 mm knitting needles, red yarn and beg. with peak, cast on 12 sts.
K 15 rows.

Next row Cast on 16 sts at beg. of row. K these 16 sts, K1, K2 tog., K1, (K2 tog.) twice, K1, K2 tog., K1—24 sts.

Next row Cast on 16 sts at beg. of row. K to end—40 sts.
K 10 rows.

Next row Inc. in every st—80 sts.
K 1 row.

Next row K2 tog. across row—40 sts.

To Shape Crown

(K6, K2 tog.) to end.
(K5, K2 tog.) to end.
(K4, K2 tog.) to end.
Cont. working in this way, knitting one less st bet. decs. on every row till 10 sts rem.
K2 tog. across row—5 sts.
Break off yarn leaving a long end. Thread it through these 5 sts.
Pull firmly and tie off.

To Make Up

Body

With right sides of the two body pieces together, sew seam down each side of the head, body and legs. Sew inner leg seams. Leave top of head and base of legs open. Turn to right side and fill firmly. With a fine running st sew across top of legs bringing front to back—this will keep the legs movable. Sew seam across top of head.

BACK-TO-FRONT

Shoes
Fold one shoe in half with right sides together, bringing cast-on and cast-off edges together. Sew side seams. Turn to right side and fill firmly. Sew cast-on and cast-off edges together. Sl. st base of leg to topside of shoe. Position carefully so that the back of the leg is in line with the back of the shoe and the shoe will point slightly outwards. Complete other shoe to match.

Arms
Fold one arm in half lengthwise with right sides together, and sew side seam and across cast-on edge. Turn to right side and fill firmly. With seam at centre underside, sew across cast-off edge. Sew this edge to side of body at beg. of shoulder shaping. Complete other arm to match.

Run lengths of yarn around waist, top of neck and wrists, pull firmly to shape and tie off securely.

Nose
Fold in half with right sides together, and sew side seam. Leave cast-on edge open. Turn to right side and fill firmly. Sl. st cast-on edge to centre of face. (*Note* Face is on the opposite side to the direction of the shoes.)

Overalls
With right sides together sew side and inner leg seams. Sew straps in position at top corners of front and back bibs. Sl. st pocket to front bib. With white yarn used double, embroider spots on patch as illustrated. Sl. st patch to right knee.

Hat
Sew seam from centre of crown to cast-on edge. Turn to right side and fill loosely. Position squarely on head and sl. st in position.

Hair
Using 12-ply yellow yarn, run long loops around back of head just under hat line. Backstitch each loop as you go. Trim to length. Make a small tuft under peak.

Face
Embroider eyes in satin stitch, mouth in backstitch and cheeks by following the stitch lines as illustrated.

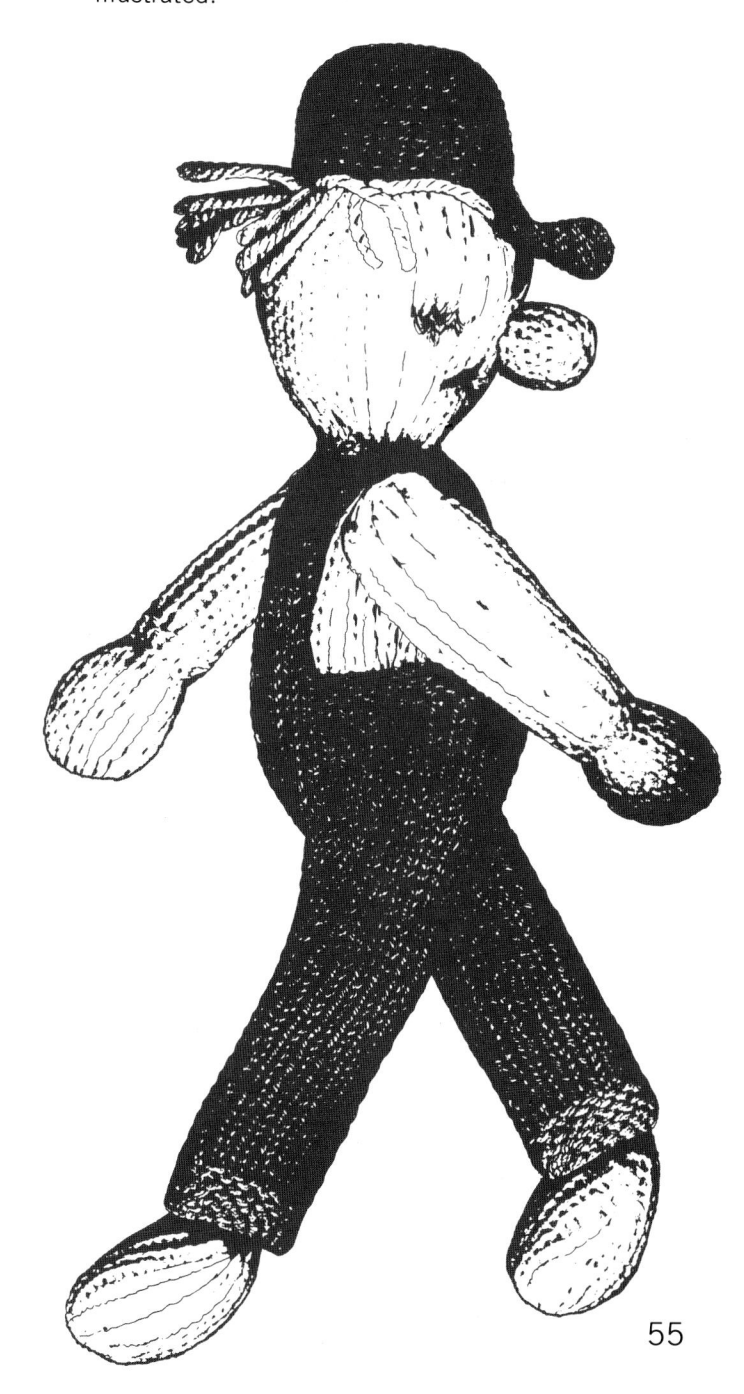

All wound up

These two adventurous characters often get themselves into tricky situations—for Inspector Gadget, his gadgets can sometimes help, and for Mr Squiggle, it's his pencil nose.

Inspector Gadget

Mr Squiggle

MR SQUIGGLE***

Description

Legs, body, arms and head are knitted in two pieces—one for the back and one for the front. Hat, nose and ears are each knitted in one piece. Eyes and mouth are embroidered. Hair is added separately. When completed he stands approx. 50 cm tall.

Mr Squiggle, the only man from the moon who can draw with his nose, arrived on earth from Crater Crescent more than thirty years ago. Every detail of this colourful toy is created with wool.

Materials

One 50 g ball green 8-ply yarn
One 50 g ball yellow 8-ply yarn
One 25 g ball black 8-ply yarn
One 25 g ball lemon 5-ply yarn
One 25 g ball red 8-ply yarn
One 25 g ball white 8-ply yarn
One 25 g ball grey 8-ply yarn
Small quantities of dark pink and light green 8-ply yarn, and green 12-ply yarn for hair
One small white button
3 stitch holders
One pair 3.25 mm knitting needles
Tapestry needle.
Polyester fibre filling

Abbreviations

See page 4.

Front

Right Leg

With 3.25 mm knitting needles, lemon yarn and beg. with the right foot, cast on 10 sts.
Working in st.st inc. at end of next row and at this same edge on every foll. row till 19 sts.
Cast off 9 sts P wise at beg. of next row—10 sts.
St.st 2 rows.
*Break off lemon yarn, and join in green and black yarns for leggings. Working in stripes of 4 rows green and 2 rows black, st.st 30 rows.**
Break yarn and leave on needle.

MR SQUIGGLE

Left Leg

With 3.25 mm knitting needles and lemon yarn, cast on 10 sts.
Working in st.st, inc. at beg. of next row and at this same edge on every foll. row till 19 sts.
P 1 row.
Cast off 9 sts at beg. of next row—10 sts.
P 1 row.
Cont. as right leg from * to **.
Do not break off yarns.
St.st 2 rows across both legs—20 sts.

To Shape Body

Next row (K1, inc. in next st) 5 times, (inc. in next st, K1) 5 times—30 sts.
Cont. in striped st.st as before for 15 rows.
Break off green and black yarns and join in yellow yarn.
Dec. at each end of next and foll. alt. rows till 24 sts rem.
P 1 row. *Do not break off yellow yarn.*

To Shape Arms

(First wind grey yarn into two small balls.)
Join in one ball of grey yarn and cast on 24 sts at beg. of row. K6. Turn.
P back.
K25 grey, and rem. K23 yellow.
Join in other ball of grey yarn and cast on 24 sts at beg. of row.
P6. Turn.
K back.

Next row P25 grey, P22 yellow, P25 grey.

Next row K26 grey, K20 yellow, K26 grey.

Next and foll. alt. rows P grey sts grey, and yellow sts yellow.
Cont. working in this way, moving each grey arm towards centre by one st on every row for a further 6 rows. (Last row should be: P29 grey, P14 yellow, P29 grey.)

Next row K6. Turn.
P back.
Cast off 30 sts at beg. of row, K to end.

Next row P6. Turn.
K back.
Cast off 30 sts P wise at beg. of row, P to end—12 sts.
Break off grey yarn and cont. in yellow only.

To Shape Neck

Dec. at each end of 3rd and foll. 4th row—8 sts rem.
St.st 5 rows.

To Shape Head

Next row Inc. K wise in every st—16 sts.

Next row (P1, inc. in next st P wise.) Rpt to end—24 sts.
St.st 30 rows.

Next row (K1, K2 tog.) to end—16 sts.

Next row P2 tog. to end—8 sts.
Break yarn, leaving a long end.
Thread it through these 8 sts and leave loose.

BACK

Work as for front, substituting white yarn for grey yarn.

EARS (*make 2*)

With 3.25 mm knitting needles, and yellow yarn, cast on 8 sts.
K 6 rows.
Dec. at each end of next two rows—4 sts.
Cast off.

HAT

With 3.25 mm knitting needles and white yarn, cast on 50 sts.
K 12 rows.

MR SQUIGGLE

Break off white yarn and join in green and black yarns.
Working in st.st and stripes of 4 rows green and 4 rows black, dec. at each end of 5th and foll. 4th rows till 10 sts rem.
P 1 row.
Break yarn leaving a long end of green, thread through these rem. 10 sts, and pull firmly. Tie off yarns

NOSE

With 3.25 mm knitting needles and red yarn, cast on 15 sts.
St.st 18 rows.
Break off red yarn, and join in dark pink yarn.
St.st 2 rows.

Next row (K3, K2 tog.) Rpt to end—12 sts.

Next row P to end.

Next row (K2, K2 tog.) Rpt to end—9 sts.

Next row P to end.

Next row (K1, K2 tog.) Rpt to end—6 sts.

Next row P to end.
Break off dark pink yarn and join in black yarn.

Next row K2 tog. across row—3 sts.

Next row P to end.
Break yarn leaving a long end.
Thread it through rem. 3 sts, pull firmly and tie off.

SMOCK

Front

With 3.25 mm knitting needles and lemon yarn, cast on 50 sts.
K 1 row.
Working in st.st beg. with a K row, dec. at each end of 3rd and foll. 4th rows till 38 sts.
P 1 row.*

To Shape Armholes

Cast off 4sts. at beg. of next 2 rows—30 sts.
Dec. at each end of next and foll. alt. rows till 14 sts rem.
P 1 row.
Leave on stitch holder.

Back

Work as front to *.

Next row Cast off 4 sts, K14. Turn.

Next row K2, P13.
Working on these 15 sts, dec. at the beg. of next and foll. alt. rows till 8 sts rem.
(Remember to start each P row with K2.)

Next row K2, P6.

Buttonhole row K2 tog., K to last 2 sts, y. fwd, K2 tog—7 sts.

Next row K2, P5.
Leave these 7 sts on stitch holder, and join yarn to rem. sts on needle. Complete this side to match—reversing shapings and omitting buttonhole.

SLEEVES (*make 2*)

To Shape Cuff

With 3.25 mm knitting needles and white yarn, cast on 2 sts.
Working in g. st, inc. at beg. of next row and at this same edge on every foll. row till 8 sts.
Break yarn and leave sts on needle.
Work another piece, reversing shaping.
Do not break yarn.

Next row K across the first 8 sts, cast on 8 sts, K across second 8 sts—24 sts.
K 4 rows.
Break off white yarn, and join in green and black yarns for sleeves.
Working in stripes of 4 rows green and 2 rows black, st.st 26 rows.

To Shape Armholes

Cast off 4 sts at the beg. of next 2 rows—16 sts.
Dec. at each end of next and foll. alt. rows till 2 sts rem.
P 1 row. K tog. Fasten off.

MR SQUIGGLE

Bow Tie

Bow Piece

With 3.25 mm knitting needles and red yarn, cast on 20 sts.
K 56 rows. Cast off.

Tie Piece

With 3.25 mm knitting needles and red yarn, cast on 80 sts.
Working in g. st, dec. at each end of next and foll. alt. rows till 74 sts rem.
K 1 row. Cast off.

To Make Up

Body

With right sides together, sew seams down each side of the head, neck, around arms, body, legs and feet. Sew seam between legs. Leave opening at top of head. Turn to right side and fill legs firmly. With a fine running stitch sew front of legs to back of legs through top black row. This will keep the legs movable. Cont. to fill body, arms, neck and head firmly.
Draw stitches together at top of head to close opening. Tie off.

Hat

With right sides together, fold in half lengthwise and sew side seam. Turn to right side. Make a small white pompon (see 'Useful Information' on page 3), and attach to end. Turn white border up and fill very loosely Slip stitch in position so that the hat sits squarely on the top of the head and the seam is at centre back. With a fine running stitch, sew along seam line and pull firmly so that the hat curves over towards the back. Tie off securely.

Hair

With 12-ply green yarn, work 3 rows of loops around back of head— backstitch each loop securely as you go. Top row should be just below the hat line and the bottom row should lie around the centre line of the head.

Ears

Slip stitch cast-on edge of each ear to side seams at exact centre of side of head.

Nose

Fold nose in half lengthwise with right sides together and sew side seams, leave cast-on edge open. Turn to right side and fill firmly. With black yarn and a long stitch embroider 6 lines along the length of the red section. Slip stitch in position at exact centre of face.

Using red yarn, embroider mouth with a fine backstitch.
Embroider eyes as illustrated.

Using red yarn and a long stitch, run 2 lines at end of each hand as illustrated.

Smock

Sew in raglan sleeves, joining front to back just above top of sleeve. Join side and sleeve seams.

To Shape Collar

With 3.25 mm knitting needles and white yarn, K up 7 sts from right back and 7 sts from right front.
K 6 rows. Cast off.
Complete the other side to match. Sew on button at back.

Bow Tie

Position bow piece over the centre of the tie piece and stitch through both pieces, catching to front of smock approx. 3 cm down from collar.
Tie tie piece round firmly, gathering the bow piece at centre.

INSPECTOR GADGET ***

Description

Legs, body and head are knitted in two main pieces, one for the back and one for the front. Arms, shoes, ears, nose, hair and hat are knitted in one piece each. Overcoat is knitted all in one piece with lapels, cuff bands, belt loops and belt knitted separately. Tie, mouth and eyes are embroidered.
When completed he stands approx. 30 cm tall.

Inspector Gadget is a real optimist through thick and thin. He gets himself into and out of lots of sticky situations not just with the help of his gadgets but also his offsiders, Penny and Brain.

Inspector Gadget

Materials

Two 50 g balls light grey 8-ply yarn
One 25 g ball dark grey 8-ply yarn
One 25 g ball blue 8-ply yarn
One 25 g ball white 8-ply yarn
One 20 g ball fawn 8-ply yarn
Small quantities black and dark brown 8-ply yarns
6 press studs
10 small white buttons
One small silver buckle
One stitch holder
One pair 3.25 mm knitting needles
Tapestry needle
Polyester fibre filling

Abbreviations

See page 4.

Back

With 3.25 mm knitting needles, blue yarn and beg. with left trouser leg, cast on 8 sts K 1 row.
Beg. with a K row st.st 30 rows.
Break yarn and leave sts on R.H. needle.
Work another leg the same. *Do not break yarn.*

Next row (Inc. in 1st.st, K6, inc. in next st.) Rpt across 2nd leg—20 sts.
Beg. with a P row st.st 15 rows.
Break off blue yarn and join in white yarn for shirt.
St.st 14 rows.

To Shape Shoulder

Cast off 3 sts at beg. of next 2 rows, then 2 sts at the beg. of foll. 2 rows—10 sts rem.
Break off white yarn and join in fawn yarn for head.*

To Shape Head

Working in st.st inc. at each end of 9th and foll. 10th rows—14 sts.
P 1 row.
Cast off 2 sts at beg. of every row till 2 sts rem. K2 tog. Fasten off.

Front

Work as for back to *

To Shape Chin

St.st 8 rows.
Place markers of coloured yarn at each end of last row.
St.st 6 rows.
Dec at each end of next row—8 sts.
St.st 3 rows.
Dec. at each end of every row till 4 sts rem.
K 1 row.

To Shape Face Piece

Working in st.st, inc. at each end of every row till 8 sts.
St.st 3 rows.
Inc. at each end of next row—10 sts.
St.st 5 rows.
Place markers of coloured yarn at each end of last row.
Inc. at each end of next and foll. 10th row—14 sts.
P 1 row.
Cast off 2 sts at beg. of every row till 2 sts rem.
K2 tog. Fasten off.

Shoes (make 2)

With 3.25 mm knitting needles and dark grey yarn, cast on 12 sts.
Working in st.st, inc. at each end of the 7th and foll. 8th row—16 sts.
St.st 5 rows.
Dec. at each end of next and foll. 8th row—12 sts.
St.st 5 rows. Cast off.

Arms (make 2)

With 3.25 mm knitting needles and choc. brown yarn, cast on 12 sts.
Inc. K wise in every st—24 sts.
Beg. with a P row, st.st 6 rows.
K 1 row.
Break off choc. brown yarn and join in white yarn for sleeve.

Inspector Gadget

Next row (K2 tog., K2.) Rpt to end of row—18 sts.
Beg. with a P row, st.st 21 rows.

To Shape Armholes
Cast off 2 sts at the beg. of next 2 rows.
Dec. at each end of every row till 2 sts rem.
K2 tog. Fasten off.

Ears (make 2)

With 3.25 mm knitting needles and fawn yarn, cast on 4 sts.
Inc. K wise in every st—8 sts.
Beg with a P row, st.st 3 rows.
Dec. in each end of next and foll. alt. row—4 sts.
P 1 row. Cast off.

Nose

With 3.25 mm knitting needles and fawn yarn, cast on 10 sts.
St.st 2 rows.

Next row K3, K2 tog., K2 tog. t.b.l., K3.
St.st 3 rows.

Next row K2, K2 tog., K2 tog. t.b.l., K2.
St.st 3 rows.
Dec. at each end of every row till 2 sts rem.
K2 tog. Fasten off.

Hair

With 3.25 mm knitting needles and black yarn, cast on 4 sts.
K 3 rows.
*Working in g. st, inc. at beg. of next and at this same edge on every foll. row till 10 sts.
Dec. at beg. of next and at this same edge on every foll. row till 4 sts rem.**
Rpt from * to ** 3 times.
K 3 rows. Cast off.

Hat

With 3.25 mm knitting needles and dark grey yarn, cast on 50 sts.

Rows 1 & 3 K.

Row 2 (K3, K2 tog.) to end—40 sts.

Row 4 (K2, K2 tog.) to end—30 sts.

Row 5 Inc. in every st—60 sts.

Row 6 K2 tog. across the row—30 sts.
Break off dark grey yarn and join in light grey yarn for hatband.
K 6 rows.
Break off light grey yarn and join in dark grey yarn.
K 4 rows.

Next row Inc. in every st—60 sts.

Next row K2 tog. across row—30 sts.

To Shape Crown

Row 1 (K1, K2 tog.) to end—20 sts.

Rows 2 & 4 K.

Row 3 K2 tog. across row—10 sts.

Row 5 K2 tog. across row—5 sts.

Row 6 K.
Break yarn, leaving a long end.
Thread it through these 5 sts and pull firmly. Tie off.

63

INSPECTOR GADGET

Overcoat

With 3.25 mm knitting needles, light grey yarn and beg. at left front, cast on 35 sts.
K 1 row.
Working in g. st, inc. at beg. of next row and at the same edge on foll. 3rd rows till 45 sts.

To Shape Left Sleeve

*K16 sts. Turn. Leave rem. 29 sts on a stitch holder.
Cast on 16 sts at beg. of row.
K12. Turn. K to end.
K14. Turn. K to end.
K16. Turn. K to end.
Cont. to work in this way, knitting 2 extra sts on each alt. row until all 32 sts have been worked.
K 1 row across all 32 sts.
K30. Turn. K to end.
K28. Turn. K to end.
K26. Turn. K to end.
Cont. to work in this way, knitting 2 fewer sts on each alt. row until the row K12. Turn. K to end has been completed.
Cast off 16 sts at beg. of next row (sl. last st back on to L.H. needle). Break yarn and leave sts on needle.
Ret. to rem. 29 sts on stitch holder and K 19 rows.
Next row K these 29 sts then 16 sts from sleeve—45 sts.**
K 19 rows.

To Shape Back Opening

Cast off 15 sts, then cast on 15 sts.
K 19 rows across all 45 sts.

To Shape Right Sleeve

Work as for left sleeve from * to **.
Dec. at beg. of next row and at this same edge on foll. 3rd rows till 35 sts rem.
K 1 row. Cast off.

To Shape Collar

With W.S. facing, pick up 16 sts up left front shaping, 21 sts across back and 16 sts down right front shaping—53 sts.
K 8 rows. Cast off.

Belt

With 3.25 mm knitting needles and dark grey yarn, cast on 75 sts.
Cast off.

Epaulettes, Cuffs, Bands and Belt Loops (make 8)

With 3.25 mm knitting needles and light grey yarn, cast on 8 sts.
Cast off.

To Make Up

Body

Firstly with right sides together fold chin section so that coloured markers meet at each side. Sew seam up each side of chin to coloured markers. Place right sides of two body pieces together and sew seam down each side of head. Be careful not to catch any chin section. Continue down each side of body and trousers to cast-on edges. Sew between legs. Leave top of head and base of trousers open. Turn to right side and fill firmly. Sew up opening at top of head.

Shoes

Fold one shoe in half with right sides together, so that cast-on and cast-off edges meet. Sew side seams. Turn to right side, fill firmly and sew cast-on and cast-off edges together. Position at base of leg so that back seam is in line with the back of the leg and shoe faces slightly outwards. Sl. st in position. Complete other shoe to match. Embroider black laces as illustrated.

Arms

Fold one arm in half lengthwise with right sides together and sew seam from cast-on edge to armhole shaping. Place seam at centre back and sew across hand seam.
Turn to right side and fill firmly. Sl. st in position so that top of arm shaping lies approx. 1 cm down from neck edge. Run a length of yarn

INSPECTOR GADGET

around wrist and pull firmly to shape glove. Complete other arm and glove to match.

Ears

Fold one ear in half lengthwise with wrong sides together and sew side seam. With seam at centre back, sew across cast-off edge at top of ear. Sl. st in position as illustrated. Complete other ear to match.

Nose

Fold in half lengthwise with right sides together and sew seam across cast-on edge. Turn to right side and fill firmly. Positioning carefully, sl. st in position as illustrated.

Hair

Sl. st cast-off and cast-on edges just above each ear, so that shapings point outwards. Sl. st top edge around back of head, easing in fullness.

Eyes, Mouth and Tie

Embroider eyes in satin stitch, mouth in backstitch and tie in satin stitch as illustrated.

Hat

With right sides together sew seam from centre of crown to cast-on edge. Turn to right side and sl. st in position around lower edge of hat band.

Overcoat

With right sides of one sleeve together, sew cast-on and cast-off edges together from end along 12 sts. With the sleeve seam at the centre sew along underarm opening. Complete other sleeve to match. Roll collar to right side and catch down at corners. Sew on front buttons as illustrated and attach press studs to inside of buttons. Attach top of epaulettes just below collar and catch ends down with buttons. Attach cuff bands in the same way. Sew belt loops to jacket, 2 at the front and 2 at the back. Sew the buckle to one end of the belt and thread through belt loops as illustrated.

OUTDOOR ADVENTURE

For Postman Pat and David the Gnome, outdoor life is always busy. Postman Pat is set in the quaint little village of Greendale while David the Gnome uses herbal remedies to look after all the gnomes and animals in Gnomeland.

The World of *David, The Gnome*

Postman Pat

Postman Pat and Jess ***

Description

Postman Pat
Legs, body and head are knitted in two pieces, one for the front and one for the back. Shoes, arms, nose, ears, jacket and hat are knitted in one piece each. Hair, eyes, spectacles, mouth, shirt and tie are embroidered. Mail sack and letter are knitted in one piece each. When completed he stands approx. 32 cm tall.

Jess
Body, head, tail, ears and paws are knitted in one piece each. White face patch is knitted separately. Mouth, eyes and nose are embroidered. When completed she stands approx. 8 cm high and is approx. 9 cm long.

Materials

Postman Pat
Two 50 g balls royal blue 8-ply yarn
One 25 g ball white 8-ply yarn
One 25 g ball black 8-ply yarn
One 25 g ball apricot 8-ply yarn
One 25 g ball brown 8-ply yarn for sack
Small quantities orange, rust, yellow and choc. brown 8-ply yarns
Two brass buttons
One stitch holder

Jess
One 25 g ball black mohair 12-ply yarn
One 25 g ball white mohair 12-ply yarn
Small quantities of green and dark apricot 8-ply yarns
One pair 3.25 mm knitting needles
Tapestry needle
Polyester fibre filling

Abbreviations
See page 4.

Postman Pat is not just a postman—he's a friend to everyone in Greendale, and they always look forward to him arriving with their letters and parcels. The likeness of this toy to Postman Pat is remarkable.

Jess is Postman Pat's cat who goes everywhere with him.

Postman Pat and Jess

Postman Pat

Body (make 2)

With 3.25 mm knitting needles, royal blue yarn and beg. with right trouser leg, cast on 24 sts.
K 16 rows.
Cast off 14 sts at the beg. of next row.
K 1 row.
Cast on 14 sts at beg. of next row.
K 15 rows. Cast off.

To Shape Shirt

With 3.25 mm knitting needles, white yarn and with R.S. facing, pick up 20 sts evenly across top of trousers.
Beg. with a P row st.st 19 rows.

To Shape Shoulders

Cast off 3 sts at beg. of next 2 rows, and 2 sts at beg. of foll. 2 rows—10 sts rem.
Break of white yarn and join in apricot yarn for head.

To Shape Head

Cont. in st.st, inc. at each end of 9th and foll. 10th rows—14 sts.
St.st 11 rows.
Cast off 2 sts at beg. of every row till 2 sts rem. K2 tog. Fasten off.

Arms (make 2)

With 3.25 mm knitting needles, apricot yarn and beg. with hand, cast on 12 sts.

Row 1 Inc. K wise in every st—24 sts.
Beg. with a P row, st.st 7 rows.
Break off apricot yarn and join in white yarn for sleeve.

Next row (K2 tog., K2) to end of row—18 sts.
St.st 15 rows.

To Shape Armholes

Cast off 2 sts at beg. of next 2 rows.
Dec. at each end of every row till 2 sts rem.
K2 tog. Fasten off.

Shoes (make 2)

With 3.25 mm knitting needles and black yarn, cast on 12 sts. Working in st.st inc. at each end of 7th and foll. 8th row—16 sts.
St.st 5 rows.
Dec. at each end of next and foll. 8th row—12 sts rem.
St.st 5 rows. Cast off.

Ears (make 2)

With 3.25 mm knitting needles and apricot yarn, cast on 8 sts.
K 1 row.
Working in g. st dec. at each end of every row till 2 sts rem. K2 tog. Fasten off.

Nose

With 3.25 mm knitting needles and apricot yarn, cast on 20 sts.

Row 1 K2 tog. across row—10 sts.
Beg. with a P row, st.st 7 rows.

Next row K2 tog. across row—5 sts rem.
Break yarn leaving a long end. Thread it through rem. 5 sts, pull firmly and tie off.

Jacket

With 3.25 mm knitting needles, royal blue yarn and beg. at left front, cast on 20 sts.
K 1 row.

Buttonhole row Inc. in 1st st, K4, y. fwd, K2 tog., K6, y. fwd, K2 tog., K5—21 sts.
K 1 row.
Working in g. st, inc. at beg. of next and foll. alt. rows till 30 sts.
K 1 row.

To Shape Left Sleeve

*K16. Turn. Leave rem. 14 sts on a stitch holder.
Cast on 8 sts at beg. of row.
K4. Turn.
K to end.
K6. Turn.

Postman Pat and Jess

K to end.
Cont. to work in this way, inc. each alt. row by 2 sts until all 24 sts have been worked.
K 1 row across all sts.
K22. Turn.
K to end.
K20. Turn.
K to end.
Cont. to work in this way, dec. each alt. row by 2 sts, until (K4, turn, K to end) has been completed.
Cast off 8 sts at beg. of row.
(Sl. last st back onto L.H. needle.)
Break yarn and leave sts on needle.
Ret. to rem. 14 sts and K 19 rows.

Next row K14, then K16 from sleeve—30 sts.**
K 40 rows.

To Shape Right Sleeve

Work right sleeve as for left sleeve from * to **.
Dec. at beg. of next and foll. alt. rows till 20 sts rem.
K 1 row. Cast off.

To Shape Collar

With W.S. facing, pick up 11 sts up left front shaping, 23 sts across back and 11 sts down right front shaping—45 sts.
K 6 rows. Cast off.

Pockets (*make 2*)

With 3.25 mm knitting needles and royal blue yarn, cast on 10 sts.
K 16 rows. Cast off.

Hat

To Shape Peak

With 3.25 mm knitting needles and black yarn, cast on 2 sts.
Working in g. st inc. at each end of next and foll. alt. rows till 16 sts.
Break off black yarn and join in royal blue yarn for band.

To Shape Band

Cast on 10 sts at beg. of row.
K these first 10 sts then work from peak (K2 tog., K1) twice, (K2 tog.) twice, (K1, K2 tog.) twice.
Cast on 10 sts at beg. of row.
K to end—30 sts.
K 4 rows.

To Shape Crown

Inc. in every st—60 sts.
K 5 rows.

Next row K50. Turn.

Next row K40. Turn.

Next row K30. Turn.

Next row K20. Turn.

Next row K15. Turn.

Next row K10. Turn.
K to end of row.
K 1 row.

Next row (K10, K2 tog.) to end.

Next row (K9, K2 tog.) to end.
Cont. in this way, working one less st bet. decs. on every row till 10 sts rem.

Next row K2 tog. across row—5 sts.
Break yarn leaving a long end.
Thread it through these 5 sts, pull firmly and tie off.

Mail Sack

With 3.25 mm knitting needles and brown yarn, cast on 50 sts.
K 40 rows.

Next row K1, (y. fwd, K2 tog.) to last st, K1.
K 7 rows. Cast off.

Letter

With 3.25 mm knitting needles and white yarn, cast on 10 sts.
St.st 7 rows, beg. with a K row.
K 1 row.
St.st 7 rows, beg. with a K row.
Cast off P wise.

To Make Up Postman Pat

Body

With the right sides of the two body pieces together, sew seam around head and down each side of the

69

Postman Pat and Jess

body and legs. Sew between legs. Leave bases of legs open. Turn to right side (turning through one of the legs) and fill firmly.

Shoes

Fold one shoe in half with right sides together, so that cast-on and cast-off edges meet. Sew side seams. Turn to right side, fill firmly and sew cast-on and cast-off edges together. Position at base of leg so that cast-on and cast-off edge are in line with back of leg and the shoe protrudes approx. 2 cm at the front. Sl. st in position. Complete other shoe to match.

Arms

Fold one arm in half lengthwise with right sides together, sew seam around hand and sleeve to armhole shaping. Turn to right side and fill firmly. Sl. st in position so that top of arm shaping lies approx. 1 cm down from neck edge. Run a length of yarn around wrist and pull firmly to shape hand. Make fingers by running lengths of yarn from end of hand approx. 1 cm to centre. Pull firmly and tie off. Complete other arm and hand to match.

Ears

Sl. st cast-on edges of ears to the seam lines on each side of the head. Position so that the top of the ear lies approx. 4 cm down from the top of the head.

Nose

Fold in half lengthwise with right sides together, and sew side seam. Turn to right side and fill firmly. With the seam to the underside and in line with the bottom of the ears, sl. st cast-on edge to centre of face.

Hair

First, with a light pencil mark top of hairline around head, approx. 1.5 cm above the top of the nose. With orange yarn sew small loops around this pencil line, backstitching each loop securely as you go. Cont. to work rows of hair down the back of the head to just below the bottom of the ears. Work a few loops in front of the ears and each side of the face as illustrated. With a fine backstitch and rust yarn, embroider spectacles, and embroider eyes and mouth in black yarn as illustrated.

With black yarn and using a long stitch embroider shirt collar. Work the shape of a tie in satin stitch.

Jacket

With the right sides of one sleeve together, match cast-on and cast-off edges. Sew sleeve seam from end along 4 sts. Sew underarm seam, matching shaping carefully. Complete other sleeve to match. Roll collar to right side and catch down at front points. Turn cast-off edge of pockets over to face front and sl. st in position as illustrated. Sew on buttons.

Hat

With right sides together sew seam from centre of crown to outer edge of band. Turn to right side. With yellow yarn, embroider emblem at centre of band as illustrated. Sl. st cast-on edge of hat to head around top hairline.

Mail Sack

Fold in half so that side edges match. Sew side and bottom seam. Turn to right side and fill loosely. Make a twisted cord (see 'Useful Information' at front of book) and thread through holes at top of sack. Pull firmly and tie. With choc. brown yarn, embroider 'MAIL' as illustrated.

Letter

Fold in half with right sides together, matching cast-on and cast-off edges. Sew side seams. Turn to right side and sew cast-on and cast-off edges together. With black thread embroider as illustrated.

POSTMAN PAT AND JESS

JESS BODY

*With 3.25 mm knitting needles, black mohair yarn and beg. at rear, cast on 12 sts.

Row 1 Inc. K wise in every st—24 sts.**

Beg. with a P row st.st 19 rows. Break off black mohair yarn and join in white mohair yarn for chest. St.st 2 rows.

Next row K2 tog. across row—12 sts.

Break yarn, leaving a long end. Thread it through rem. sts, pull firmly and tie off.

HEAD

Work as for body from * to **. St.st 11 rows.

Next row K2 tog. across row—12 sts. Break yarn, leaving a long end. Thread it through rem. sts, pull firmly and tie off.

PAWS (make 2 black, 2 white)

Cast on 5 sts, st.st 10 rows, cast off.

TAIL

With 3.25 mm knitting needles and black mohair yarn, cast on 16 sts.

Row 1 K2 tog. across row—8 sts. Beg. with a P row, st.st 7 rows. Break off black mohair yarn and join in white mohair yarn. St.st 4 rows.

Break yarn, leaving a long end. Thread it through these 8 sts, pull firmly and tie off.

EARS (make 2)

With 3.25 mm knitting needles and black mohair yarn, cast on 6 sts. K 2 rows.

Working in g. st, dec. at each end of next and foll. alt. rows till 2 sts rem. K2 tog. Fasten off.

FACE PATCH

With 3.25 mm knitting needles and white mohair yarn, cast on 2 sts. Working in g. st, inc. at each end of every row till 8 sts. K 5 rows. Dec. at each end of every row till 2 sts rem. K2 tog. Fasten off.

TO MAKE UP JESS

Body
Fold in half lengthwise with right sides together, and sew side seam. Turn to right side and fill firmly.* Run a length of yarn around cast-on edge and pull firmly to close gap. Tie off.

Head
Work as for body to *. Placing the body seam to the underside and the head seam to the back, sl. st cast-on edge of the head to the body. Position carefully just above the chest piece.

Paws
Fold one paw in half with right sides together, matching cast-on edge to cast-off edge. Sew side seams. Turn to right side, fill firmly and sew cast-on and cast-off edges together. Complete other three paws to match. Embroider white paws with black yarn and black paws with white yarn as illustrated. Sl. st back and side seams of paws to underside of body, white paws to the front and black paws to the back.

Tail
Work as for body to *. Sl. stitch cast-on edge to back of body.

Ears
With white yarn, embroider front of ears as illustrated. Sl. stitch cast-on edges to top of head.

Face Patch
Sl. stitch to front of face, matching cast-on edge to top of chest piece.

Embroider eyes in green and black satin stitch, nose in dark apricot satin stitch, and mouth in black backstitch as illustrated.

DAVID THE GNOME AND LISA

David is a gnome and is very wise. He is a keen gardener and makes lots of his medicines from plants which he collects. You'll see how his size adds to his charm when you knit him up!

Lisa is David's wife. She loves to collect lots of berries to make delicious jams and tarts. She completes this quaint little pair who will sit snuggly on your window sill.

DAVID THE GNOME AND LISA**

DESCRIPTION

David
Legs, body and head are knitted in two pieces, one for the front and one for the back. Arms, hat, beard, ears and belt are knitted in one piece each. Face is embroidered.

Lisa
Body, arms and hat made as for David. Scarf, skirt and apron are knitted in one piece each.

Both David and Lisa stand approx. 23 cm high to top of hat.

MATERIALS

David
One 20 g ball blue 8-ply yarn
One 20 g ball olive green 8-ply yarn
One 20 g ball red 8-ply yarn
One 20 g ball white 8-ply yarn
One 20 g ball apricot 8-ply yarn
One 20 g ball fawn 8-ply yarn
Small quantities orange, yellow, black and crimson 8-ply yarns

Lisa
One 20 g ball mid-blue 8-ply yarn
One 20 g ball pale-blue 8-ply yarn
One 20 g ball white 8-ply yarn
One 20 g ball apricot 8-ply yarn
One 20 g ball crimson 8-ply yarn
Small quantities, black, red and brown 8-ply yarns
One pair 3.25 mm knitting needles
Tapestry needle
Polyester fibre filling

ABBREVIATIONS
See page 4.

DAVID FRONT

With 3.25 mm knitting needles, fawn yarn and beg. with right boot, cast on 16 sts.
St.st 5 rows.

Next row P2 tog. across row—8 sts.
St.st 4 rows.
*Break off fawn yarn and join in olive green yarn for trousers.
K 6 rows.
Break yarn and leave sts on needle. Work another leg the same. *Do not break yarn.*

To Shape Body

Next row (Inc. in 1st st, K6, inc. in next st.) Rpt across 2nd leg—20 sts.
K 9 rows.
Break off olive green yarn and join in blue yarn for jacket.
K 10 rows.
Dec. at each end of next and foll. alt. row—16 sts.
K 1 row.
Dec. at each end of every row till 8 sts rem.
Break off blue yarn and join in apricot yarn for head.

To Shape Head

Next row Inc. K wise in every st—16 sts.
Beg. with a P row, st.st 13 rows.

Next row K2 tog. across row—8 sts.
Cast off P wise.

BACK

With 3.25 mm knitting needles, fawn yarn and beg. with left boot, cast on 8 sts.
St.st 10 rows.
Complete as for front from *.

ARMS (*make 2*)

With 3.25 mm knitting needles, apricot yarn and beg. with hand, cast on 8 sts.
Inc. K wise in every st—16 sts.
Beg. with a P row, st.st 5 rows.
Break off apricot yarn and join in blue yarn for sleeve.

David the Gnome and Lisa

Next row (K2 tog., K1) twice, (K2 tog.) twice, (K1, K2 tog.) twice—10 sts.
K 13 rows.

To Shape Armholes

Cont. in g. st, dec. at each end of next and foll. alt. rows till 2 sts rem. K2 tog. Fasten off.

Bottom of Jacket and Belt (*knitted in one piece*)

With 3.25 mm knitting needles and blue yarn, cast on 60 sts.
K 5 rows.
Break off blue yarn and join in orange yarn for belt.

Next row (K2 tog., K1) to end of row—40 sts.
K 3 rows. Cast off.

Hat

With 3.25 mm knitting needles and red yarn, cast on 41 sts.
K 3 rows.

Next row (K8, K2 tog.) to last st, K1.
K 3 rows.

Next row (K7, K2 tog.) to last st, K1.
K 3 rows.
Cont. working in this way, knitting one less st between decs. on every 4th row till 9 sts rem.
K 3 rows.

Next row K2 tog. to last st, K1—5 sts.
K 3 rows.
Break yarn, leaving a long end. Thread it through these 5 sts, pull firmly and tie off.

Beard

With 3.25 mm knitting needles and white yarn, cast on 18 sts.
Inc. K wise in every st—36 sts.
Working in g. st, dec. at each end of next and foll. alt. rows till 2 sts rem. K2 tog. Fasten off.

Ears (*make 2*)

With 3.25 mm knitting needles and apricot yarn, cast on 4 sts.
Inc. K wise in every st—8 sts.
Beg. with a P row, st.st 5 rows.

Next row K2 tog. across row. Cast off P wise.

To Make Up David

Body

With right sides together, sew seam down each side of the head, body and legs. Sew inner leg seams. Leave top of head and bottom of boots open.
Placing leg seams together, sew across cast-on edges at base of each boot.
Turn to right side and fill firmly. Sew cast-off edges at top of head together.

Bottom of Jacket and Belt

Fold right sides together and sew back seam. Run a length of orange yarn around the cast-off row of belt, leave ends loose. Sl. up over legs till top row of belt meets the bottom row of blue jacket. Pull the yarn firmly and tie off. Embroider buckle with a double length of yellow yarn.

Arms

Fold the right sides of one arm together lengthwise and sew seam across cast-on edge of hand and down length of hand and arm to armhole. Turn to right side and fill firmly. Sl. st armhole to side of body, matching top point to neck edge. Run a length of yarn around wrist and pull firmly to shape. Complete other arm to match.

Ears

Fold wrong sides of one ear together and sew side seam, placing seam at centre back. Sew across cast-off edge at top of ear. Sl. st cast-on edge to neck edge slightly behind side seam. Complete other ear to match.

DAVID THE GNOME AND LISA

Beard
Sl. st cast-on edge to face, matching side edges to side seams.

Hair
Run loops of white yarn around back of head level with the top of the ears. Backstitch each loop as you go. Trim to length.

Hat
Fold right sides together and sew seam from tip to cast-on edge. Turn to right side and fill loosely. With seam at centre back, position hat over hair and top side edges of beard. Sl. st in position.

Face
Embroider nose, mouth, eyes, cheeks, moustache and eyebrows as illustrated.

LISA FRONT AND BACK
Work as for David using mid-blue yarn for boots, apricot yarn for legs and body, and white yarn for blouse.

ARMS
Work as for David using white yarn for sleeves.

HAT
Work as for David using mid-blue yarn.

SKIRT
With 3.25 mm knitting needles and pale blue yarn, cast on 80 sts.
K 35 rows.

Next row K2 tog. across row—40 sts.
Cast off.

SCARF
With 3.25 mm knitting needles and crimson yarn, cast on 34 sts.
Inc. K wise in every st—68 sts.
Working in g. st, dec. at each end of every row till 2 sts rem.
K2 tog. Fasten off.

APRON
With 3.25 mm knitting needles and white yarn, cast on 24 sts.
K 5 rows.
Join in brown yarn and K2 rows.
Break off brown yarn and K a further 18 rows white.

Next row K2 tog. across row—12 sts.
Cast off.

TO MAKE UP LISA
Complete body and arms as for David.

Skirt
Fold right sides together and sew side seam. Turn to right side and run a length of pale blue yarn around cast-off edge. Leave ends loose. With seam at centre back pull skirt up over legs and body to armholes. Pull yarn firmly and tie off.

Apron
Make two lengths of twisted cord and sew one to each top corner of apron. (*See* 'Useful Information' on page 3 for making a twisted cord.) Tie around waist.
Embroider blouse as illustrated.

Scarf
Sew points at each end of cast-on edge together. Run a length of yarn from this centre point around outer edge of scarf, leave ends loose. Position scarf over head with centre point under chin and sl. st cast-on edge in position. Pull the loose ends gently to fold edge under. Tie off securely.

Hat
Complete as for David and position over scarf as illustrated. Sl. st in position.

Face
Embroider nose, mouth, eyes, eyebrows, cheeks and hair as illustrated.

DAISY

... continued from page 28

FACE PATCH

With 3.25 mm knitting needles and mauve yarn, cast on 4 sts.
K 5 rows.
Inc. at each end of next and foll. 6th rows till 8 sts.
K 1 row.
Inc. at each end of next and foll. alt. rows till 14 sts.
K 1 row.
Dec. at each end of next and foll. alt. rows till 8 sts rem., then at each end of foll. 6th rows till 2 sts rem.
K2 tog. Fasten off.

NOSE PIECE

With 3.25 mm knitting needles and mauve yarn, cast on 2 sts.
Working in g. st inc. at each end of every row till 8 sts.
K 2 rows.
Dec. at each end of every row till 4 sts rem. Cast off.

BACK PATCH (*make 2*)

With 3.25 mm knitting needles and mauve yarn, cast on 4 sts.
Working in g. st inc. at each end of next and foll. alt. rows till 10 sts.
K 1 row.
Inc. at each end of next and every foll. row till 20 sts.
K 5 rows.
Dec. at each end of every row till 12 sts rem.
K 2 rows.
Dec. at each end of every row till 2 sts rem. K2 tog. Fasten off.

TO MAKE UP

Tail

With wrong sides together, join side seam down length of tail.
Sl. st cast on edge to body at end of centre seam. Make a tassel by threading short lengths of yarn through the end and tying round securely.

Ears

Sl. st cast-on edge of one ear piece to the side of the head approx. 3 cm down from the centre seam, and approx. 4 cm from front seam. Complete other ear to match.

Horns

Sew side seam as for tail, and attach to head approx. 1 cm in front of the top of each ear.

Udder

With right sides together sew side seam. Turn to right side and fill firmly. Sl. st in position slightly forward of the back legs and with the seam at centre back.

Teats

Sew side seams as for tail and attach to udder as illustrated.

Face Patch

Sl. st in position with cast-on edge just meeting the tip of the underside body piece and fitting evenly under horns and over head.

Nose Piece

Sl. st in position with cast-off edge uppermost and just covering the bottom of the face patch.

Attach eyes on either side of face patch as illustrated.
With black yarn embroider eyelashes by making three small loops over the top of the eyes and backstitch down securely. Cut and trim to length. Embroider nostrils in black satin stitch and mouth in long stitch as illustrated.

Back Patches

Sl. st one back patch in position towards front of one side of body and the other towards the back on the other side of the body, placing cast-on edge down.

Acknowledgments

Thank you to the Knitters' Guild of NSW Incorporated for their assistance in approving the knitted toys.

Thank you to the children who appear in the photographs (from left to right):
Cover: Rita Naddaf
Play School: Cameron Trevail, Madeline Gerrard and Cordelia Chiang
Johnson & friends: Timmy Denshire-Key
Raggy Dolls: Rita Naddaf
Mr Squiggle and Inspector Gadget: Daniel Zrinski
Postman Pat and Jess, David the Gnome and Lisa: Scott and Katy Brownless

Hands doing knitting: Jeanette Smith

Thanks to Jill and Robert Lore for use of their home for photography.

Permission for the characters to appear has been granted by their owners:
Johnson & Friends characters © Film Australia Pty Limited
Raggy Dolls © Boxtree Ltd 1991
The Raggy Dolls is a Trademark of Yorkshire Television Ltd
© Melvyn Jacobson Productions Ltd
Mr Squiggle © Norman Hetherington Puppets
Inspector Gadget © DIC/FR3, 1991
Postman Pat & Jess © Woodland Animations Ltd 1991
David the Gnome & Lisa © Uniboek N.B./B.R.B. Internacional, S.A. 1985/1991. All rights reserved.

Published by ABC Enterprises for the
AUSTRALIAN BROADCASTING CORPORATION
GPO Box 9994 Sydney NSW 2001

Copyright © text: Robyn Earl-Peacock, 1992
Copyright © Australian Broadcasting Corporation, 1992
First published 1992
Reprinted limp 1995, 1996 (twice)
All rights reserved. No part of this publication may be reproduced, stored in a retrieval system or transmitted in any form or by any means electronic, mechanical, photocopying, recording or otherwise, without the prior written permission of the Australian Broadcasting Corporation

National Library of Australia
Cataloguing-in-Publication entry
Earl-Peacock, Robyn.
  The ABC for kids book of knitted toys.
    ISBN 0 7333 0218 1
    ISBN 0 7333 0250 5 (limp)
  1. Knitting. 2. Soft toy making. I. Australian Broadcasting Corporation. II. Title.

745.5924

Photography by Ken Dolling
Edited by Virginia Harper
Designed by Felicity Meyer
Set in 10/12 pt Trade Gothic by Caxtons Pty Ltd, Adelaide
Colour separations by General Graphic Arts
Printed in Hong Kong by Quality Printing Ltd.
The toys in this book are based on characters seen on ABC TV.